*"George Jerjian is a genius at making
and time again."*

Katarina Hanssens Carlsson
International Business-Vision Consultant and Trainer,
Stockholm, Sweden

*"There is no one more qualified to write on the topic: George
Jerjian lives a life that exudes gratitude for all of life's gifts."*

John Williamson Rick III
Fundraising Consultant, St. Louis, Missouri, USA

*"George's compelling writing and his raw openness and honesty
simplifies a very complex subject matter and it is clear that
he speaks from true experience... most importantly, from his
heart. **Spirit of Gratitude** is a must read."*

Susan Hum
Mind Mastery & Success Coach, CCF, Montreal, Canada

*"**Spirit of Gratitude** is a real page turner, marvellously uplifting,
with humour, education and insight, as well as emotive personal
tales, as George eloquently describes a state of being which can
and does have a wonderful impact on our lives. It's a book I
will surely be sharing with others."*

Antony Haynes
Nutritional Therapist, Author, Teacher, London, England

*"Open your heart and embrace the simple lessons taught on the
pages of this book. Envelope yourself in the cocoon of gratitude,
and watch the beautiful butterfly, of your authentic self, emerge.
This book is the perfect blueprint to show you how."*

Kim Griffith
Author, *Gifted*, Denver, Colorado, USA

"As a skilled wordsmith George Jerjian combines his profound experiences with profound knowledge. Seek and you will find this book reveals the key to a joyful present and how to meet your challenges in life."

Johanna Otto-Erley
Brand Strategist and Personal Growth Consultant,
Nurenberg, Germany

"Through his own journey, George masterfully helps you understand gratitude as a transformative and powerful tool that is available to all of us."

Matthew J. Curfman, CFP®
President & Co-Owner, Richmond Brothers, Inc.
Michigan, USA

*"**Spirit of Gratitude** is full of heart and feeling. George Jerjian is an articulate author, who encapsulates the essence of gratitude through his stories, personal experiences, and well-researched ideas from thought leaders. Everyone who reads this book will come away uplifted."*

Rachael Downie
Proctor Gallagher Consultant, Tasmania, Australia

"The timing of this book couldn't be better in these "times of entitlement", and not just for the younger generation, but for all of us. I am glad to embrace all opportunities and meet all adversity with the knowledge that this is just part of the journey."

Dr. Richard Sibthorpe
Medical Practitioner, London, England

"George Jerijan has a gift for telling stories that naturally connect our hearts to a divine wisdom that we all need to embrace in order to experience true significance and success in life."

Christine Wendl
Business Strategist, International Speaker, Author,
Munich, Germany

FOREWORD BY
PROFESSOR SHEILA THE BARONESS HOLLINS

Spirit of Gratitude

CRISES ARE OPPORTUNITIES

With gratitude

GEORGE JERJIAN

Permission should be addressed in writing George Jerjian at george@spiritofgratitude.com

Editor: Sigrid Macdonald
Book Magic
http://bookmagic.biz

Cover and Book Design: Anne Karklins
annekarklins@gmail.com

ISBN-13: 978-1-989161-15-9
ISBN-10: 1989161154

To all my mentors, living and dead,
with Gratitude.

CONTENTS

FOREWORD
BY
PROFESSOR SHEILA THE BARONESS HOLLINS

George seemed quite shy on first meeting and almost apologetic as he recounted his life's journey to me. He emerged as a deeply spiritual man, grounded in reality and yet present to something transcendent – a God-seeking man, not a proselytising one.

In *Spirit of Gratitude*, George's 10th book, he gently explores whether when we rely on our intuition, we are simply giving headspace to unconscious processes and thoughts, or more profoundly are allowing ourselves to listen to God. This is a spiritual memoir in which George has revisited many seminal moments in his life following a 30-day silent retreat.

Gratitude, the virtue named in the book's title, makes an appearance in Chapter 6 with an intensely personal account of his own perceived imminent death, which fortunately turned out to be a false alarm. His gratitude for the opportunity this shocking episode presented seems to have been a turning point in a life complicated by historical and current day emigration, by family separation and grief, by being a victim of corruption, but so importantly a life sustained by the faithfulness of a long marriage.

For me his own ideas about gratitude resonate with my writings about the evidence based 'things' we need to do in our lives to promote our own mental and spiritual health and wellbeing. Giving to, and welcoming gifts from others, are two of the 5 a day for mental wealth.

George also talks about forgiveness suggesting that forgiveness is a decision rather than a feeling. This reminds me of the Marriage Encounter approach to love, which describes love as a decision too. Both love and forgiveness are about relationships and both are rather mysterious. I wrote and spoke about forgiveness after my daughter was assaulted and paralysed. I did feel enormous compassion for the suspect, especially as he was clearly a man experiencing a mental disorder at the time and died by his own hand soon afterwards. I still find it hard to forgive the newspaper who published an article misquoting me and titled 'She can't forgive' because I had said in a radio programme that only God had the power to truly forgive. Experiences such as this have certainly strengthened me and given me the confidence to speak out about things which I now see more clearly. I am so grateful that my daughter survived and lives a fulfilled life. Sometimes extraordinary events truly become extraordinary opportunities for growth.

There are many gems in the book – including ideas to inspire and encouragement to persevere.

I particularly enjoyed the chapter on 'Persistence' and George's account of Napoleon Hill's four steps to develop the 'habit of persistence'.

This book may help you to 'change the way you look at things' and in so doing, as George stresses time and again, change the things you look at. This is not a book to skim, but one to relax with and to reflect on, in your own unique journey of discovery and desire.

Sheila Hollins
London, August 2018

INTRODUCTION

Spirit of Gratitude is about my life journey, threading the challenges I have faced. These challenges have not only defined my life, but they have also acted as a springboard to new lives for me. I am so happy and grateful for all my challenges, because they were a catalyst to push me to grow. In retrospect, it is now clear that these challenges, these obstacles were my path – my life.

Why did I choose this title: *Spirit of Gratitude*? In the traditional sense, I have always been grateful for my blessings, yet now, I am acutely aware that being grateful is essential to my happiness, my life, and my work. This is because gratitude is the foundation of happiness and the key to success. The author of *The Science of Getting Rich*, Wallace D. Wattles, wrote:

"A grateful mind continually expects good things, and expectation becomes faith. The reaction of gratitude upon one's mind produces faith... and without a living faith you cannot get rich by the creative method."

Put another way, when one is grateful for the things we already have, we are in a high vibration, we become a magnet for our own good, and we attract more good things to ourselves. In her book and film, *The Secret*, Rhonda Byrne wrote:

"Gratitude is a powerful process for shifting your energy and bringing more of what you want into your life. Be grateful for what you already have and you will attract more good things."

"The root of joy is gratefulness," writes Brother David Steindl-Rast, OSB, a Benedictine monk and author of *Gratefulness, The Heart of Prayer*. "We notice that joyful people are grateful and suppose that they are grateful for their joy. But the reverse is true: their joy springs from gratefulness. If one has all the good luck in the world, but takes it for granted, it will not give one joy. It is gratitude that makes us joyful."

I have spent all my life as a marketer, writer, speaker, and lately, as a coach; in a nutshell, I have always been a communicator, a sharer – (from the Latin root of the verb *communicare*, meaning to "share"). I wrote this book because I wanted to share my life experiences with my clients, prospects, and the world at large so that you might derive value and benefit from being grateful for everything in your lives.

The purpose of my stories is to engage the audience and to pique their interest to identify their real challenges, their crises, perceive them for the benefit, the opportunities, that they are, and discover or rediscover their life purpose.

I am so happy and grateful to share with you my stories, and as you read this book, I wish you much joy in your journey of self-discovery. May gratitude, through its magnetic force, draw joyous people and events to you.

1

BE YOURSELF

"To be yourself in a world that is constantly trying to make you something else is the greatest accomplishment."

Ralph Waldo Emerson

End of My World

The first defining moment in my early life, that I can remember, was in 1965, when my parents sent me to Assumption House, a Catholic boarding school in Ramsgate, a seaside town in the county of Kent, in England. I was ten years old. I had spent my early years in sunny Sudan, swimming every weekend at the Armenian club in Khartoum. I ate tasty food at home, prepared by our cook, Ahmed, and I enjoyed the company of my childhood friends at school. My parents told me that this move was good for me. In hindsight, I know it was, but at that age, it was the end of the world, as I had known it. By 1970, most of my school friends and their families had immigrated to the US, Canada, and Australia.

At boarding school, day after day, I yearned to see the sun hidden behind a curtain of clouds; it seemed to have emerged less than a few dozen times a year. I yearned for Ahmed's mouth-watering food as opposed to English food, which was so bad, I am certain that the English created table manners as a way to divert attention. I also yearned to swim and bathe in a pool, rather than immerse my body in an old-fashioned tub in a freezing bathroom. By nature, I was aware that I was a chameleon, blending with my environment, so as not to attract unnecessary attention. Yet, even though I was an outsider and an extrovert, it was essential for me to integrate, and I had a need to belong. There was no choice; it was survival, and I would survive. I made friends. I played football, rugby, and tennis, though I did not excel, and I even enjoyed becoming familiar with the natural beauty of Kent, the garden of England, the oak and apple trees, the endless green landscape, and white cliffs of Dover, and the wild, foamy waters of the English Channel. At the age of thirteen, I took entrance exams for Douai School, and I managed to scrape past the 60% mark on all subjects, including English, much to my surprise.

Jam Delight

In September 1968, I traveled with my mother by train from Paddington Station in London to Douai School. We arrived in the early afternoon in Woolhampton, a small village in the county of Berkshire, located between the cities of Reading and Newbury. After I settled into my dormitory, a very large, cold hall, with some fifty beds, I said goodbye to my mother stoically at the school entrance, and I saw her taxi vanish down the hill. I wanted to tell her that I yearned to go home with her, but I couldn't say it so as not to disappoint or upset her.

A few hours after her departure, I was sitting at the dining room table eating my supper when I felt a painful sting on my cheek and then saw an opened *Dairylea* triangle cheese drop on my plate. I looked up and saw the boy who had thrown the cheese, laughing his head off. I did not react.

I kept my anger under control and continued eating my supper, as though that was the end of that matter. I kept my focus on a round Pyrex dish of strawberry jam, which was in front of me. I waited about twenty minutes, and then I picked up the dish of jam, rose from my bench, slowly walked behind the perpetrator and, turning, placed the dish firmly over his head.

For some reason, which to this day I cannot understand, pandemonium broke out; all the boys started to throw things at each other. The late Fr. Augustine, who was in charge, rushed toward our table, his index finger jabbing the air, shouting, "You, you, you, and you, go to my office at once!" Eight boys, including me, made our way to his office, and we waited in anxious silence. Thirty long minutes later, Fr. Augustine appeared and swooshed into his office. I was one of the first into his office, and he opened a cupboard, revealing a dozen canes of different widths. "Choose your cane," he said matter-of-factly, as he looked at some papers on his desk. Deciding which might hurt the least, I chose the thinnest. When the cane hit my buttocks and lower legs, the stinging pain was so excruciatingly painful that I felt my eyes popping out of their sockets. Later, I discovered from my classmates that I could not have made a worse choice of cane.

Twilight Trauma

In the large dormitory for the new boys, the fifty beds were laid out all around the perimeter of the large hall, and there was also one row of beds in the middle area of the hall. My bed was located in the middle area; it was the last one in that middle row. One night in that first semester, a night I can scarcely forget, I woke up in the middle of the night, feeling pain all over. I opened my eyes to discover that four boys were punching me all over my head and body. I curled up into a ball until the assault ended. The following nights,

I did not sleep well, wondering whether another attack was imminent. The fear that it might happen again was far worse than the actual beating. This twilight trauma had embedded itself into my subconscious mind. This constant, nagging fear exhausted me mentally, and I was falling into a depression. I was unhappy; in fact, I was so miserable, I wanted to explode.

One morning, I woke up with a spirit of determination. I have no idea why or how, but I swore to myself that enough was enough. I could no longer live in fear. Why should I live this way? This was no life. I made my mind up that I would fight back and not allow myself to be afraid or depressed. I would fight back and push fear out of my life. I would be joyful and powerful. I decided to take action. I felt a surge of confidence, happiness, and power. I went to the library, where I trawled through the dictionary looking for offensive or insulting words that I could use to diminish my opponents psychologically. I would use words such as "bubonic vermin," "diabolic," and "imbecile" and enjoy the look of shock and surprise on their faces. My plan worked flawlessly. Those four boys left me alone. From this point onward, I was in charge of my life and no longer afraid. I would follow Dante's instruction; I would follow my own star.

So Why Is It Important to Be Yourself?

Because in the wise words of Oscar Wilde, "Everybody else is already taken."

While it is important to be yourself, it is also so much easier. Yet, most people are too embarrassed to be themselves, so over time, they create an alter ego that is strong enough to withstand what life may throw at them.

In January 2016, having experienced a challenging time in my life, with no apparent way out of my predicament, I decided to go on a thirty day silent retreat to St Beuno's Jesuit Spirituality Center, in North Wales, to seek answers. After a fortnight of deep silence, I was able to peel away all my alter egos and to finally allow my vulnerable self, my true self, to emerge. It was a difficult journey, but it was a most rewarding experience. I am now not only in touch with my true feelings but also in touch with my true self. My life has meaning and integrity.

Springing As a Water Fountain

We make life difficult for ourselves. We do not need to try hard or strain ourselves. We just need to get out of our own way and let ourselves be.

Thomas Troward, an English author and former judge in British-administered India, wrote several books including *The Hidden Power*, in which he wrote that we are part of a Universal Source, which he calls 'Essence of Life,' so all we have to do is allow it to rise to the surface. He uses a wonderful analogy and writes that we do not have to make it rise any more than an engineer who sinks a bore-pipe for an artesian well has to make the water rise in it. The water does that by its own energy, springing as a water fountain a hundred feet into the air. In much the same way, we will find that the fountain of this Universal Source is ready to spring up in ourselves, inexhaustible and continually increasing in its flow, much as Jesus taught over two thousand years ago to the Samaritan woman at the well.

This vast infinity of living power is enough to satisfy all our desires, and it is already in us now. It only awaits our recognition for it to be manifested. It is not the Universal Source which has to grow, because that is eternally perfect in itself; but it is our recognition of it that has to grow, and this growth cannot be forced. It must come by a natural process. The important thing to recognize is that we must stop ourselves from pursuing something, which for the time being, we cannot be naturally. A rose opens up its petals by itself naturally; if forced, it will die.

We limit ourselves when we try to control the result that we seek. We should not aim at having or making something but to express all that we are. The expressing will grow when we realize the treasures that are ours already and contemplate the beauty, the positive side, of all that we are now. When we do this, we will be shocked at the possibilities in ourselves as we are. When we start to work on whatever we find positive and forget any negative thoughts, the right road will open up before us, leading us to the development of powers that we never knew we had and happiness that we never expected.

To truly know yourself is the most important skill you can ever possess. You just don't have to try hard anymore. When you know who you are, you know what you need to do, instead of looking for permission from others to do what you already know you ought to do. Practicing this philosophy allows you to bypass so much frustration caused by putting time into the wrong things. Yes, life is supposed to be full of trial and error, but this lets you find the best areas to experiment with. Once you know yourself, and realize who you really are and not who you want to be, you will become more confident, you will understand your purpose, and you will finally see where you and your specific gifts fit into the bigger picture. To truly know yourself is the most important skill you can ever possess, so what are you waiting for?

Returning to my memories of Douai School, to this day, I do not remember the names of the boys who beat me up in the middle of the night. It doesn't really matter now; it's probably a good thing because what they did is forgiven and forgotten. Perhaps the memory of who they were was erased when I rejected the fear that they had caused. In any event, I often think of the boys at Douai, friends and adversaries, and I am so grateful for their friendship and their challenges, because, without them, I would not be the person I am today. I salute them with the old boys' salutation: *Ad Multos Annos!*

2

FAITH

"Faith is to believe what you do not as yet see.
The reward for this faith is to see what you believe."

St Augustine

A Hard Landing

In the summer of 1973, at the age of eighteen, I left Douai School, after five years of boarding there. I can still hear the song and the lyrics of Alice Cooper's "School's out for summer, school's out forever." Like all my classmates, I was very keen to leave to explore the world and all its promises and to taste the freedom of the 1960s revolution. I imagined that life was there for the taking, and nothing was going to stop me. I was an Aquarian living in the Age of Aquarius, and this was my destiny. But life was to deal me a different set of cards.

In 1976, I started working in my father's successful import-export business in the Sudan. My father had built it over a fifty-year span and, being the eldest son, I was in line to succeed him. Within a month of working in the business, I knew I was in the wrong business and the wrong country. In the past, when I had visited the Sudan on school holidays, I always had a wonderful time, because of shared experiences with my friends from Khartoum, who also went to boarding school and university in the UK. These friends no longer lived in Khartoum, so the place was not the same for me. My feelings for a girl called Jane, the sister of my best friend, Alex, also complicated matters. Jane and I had been going out together, for a time, and I had grown very fond of her. That same year, Jane had decided to study nursing in Edinburgh; part of me was happy for her, but another part was unhappy about our separation.

My mother convinced me to stay and work in the Sudan for two years, and if, after that period I still wanted to leave, I would have my parents' blessing. I stayed the two full years, working to improve my father's business, but my heart was not in the business. As I prepared to leave, I realized that I could not return to England because as a Sudanese national, I needed a work permit to work in the UK. I discovered later that if I had made an application for a British passport before I had left the UK in 1976, I would have received one. I was able to return to the UK, but only as a visitor, not a permanent resident. My father, being the generous and selfless person that he was, used his connections in London to find me a job at a merchant bank, which applied for my work permit.

London Calling

In early summer of 1978, I made my way to London to my new work. I reconnected with Jane and tried to make a go of it, but in the time apart, we had both changed, and I was having difficulty accepting it. In August, my grandmother died in our summer home in France, with my mother at her side but not her favorite grandson. In November that year, just as my work permit came through, I received a phone call from Jane telling me that Alex, who was working as a civil engineer on a British building project in Somalia, was involved in a car accident with a military truck. He was killed instantly. Naively, I thought at the time that Alex's death would bring us together, but the writing was on the wall; it's just that I couldn't see it then.

That same month, I started work for Tennant Guaranty Ltd, a merchant bank in the City of London. Two years later, I left them to join my uncle, George Kassabian, at Citadel Commercial, an export finance company in London. From my uncle, I learned a great deal about the importance of trust, the export process, and congeniality to win over and keep customers. The truth was that I was unhappy in my work and my personal life, yet I seemed paralyzed, unable to close this chapter in my life and move on.

I was depressed, and on my doctor's recommendation, I visited a psychiatrist. After discovering the cause of my anxieties, he advised me to make the hard decisions or face a deepening of my depressions, which would result in my having to take lithium tablets for the rest of my life. I realized this was the end of the road for me. Nothing good could come out of persistence in this matter. My survival instinct kicked in: I decided to make my decisions and make them without further delay.

I had wanted to marry Jane because I did not want to lose her nor the precious shared memories of our youth in Khartoum. However, I knew that if I married her, I was not ready yet, and I would resent her for stopping me from my ambitions. A week later, I met with Jane and, sitting in my car, I told her as gently as I could that I could not go on anymore, and I had to end our relationship. What we wanted from life, and from each other, were diametrically opposed. The pain of leaving her was so deep, I have no words to describe it. As my misery and despair increased, I walked for hours aimlessly and, in the early evening, found myself outside the Roman Catholic Church of Our Lady of the Rosary, not far from where I lived at the time. I went to the front porch of the church, pulled the door open, and entered. There was not a soul in there. I walked down the aisle to the altar rails, and I fell on my knees and prayed to our Lord for help. I was twenty-three. That night, I emerged from that church with a deep faith that I would find what I was seeking in this life.

So, What Has Faith Got to Do with It?

The emotions of faith, love, and sex are the most powerful of all the major positive emotions. In his book *Think and Grow Rich*, Napoleon Hill writes: "When the three are blended, they have the effect of "coloring" the vibration of thought in such a way that it instantly reaches the subconscious mind, where it is changed into its spiritual equivalent, the only form that induces a response from Infinite Intelligence."

The battle I faced was a spiritual one, an internal and lonely battle.

Despite being emotionally numb, I needed to draw from this deep well of faith. I wanted to pursue my dream of going to the United States. Ever since I had studied American history, the American War of Independence, the US Constitution, and the Bill of Rights, I had fallen in love with America. The fervor of this love affair had also been fanned by the music of my adolescence – The Beach Boys, Simon and Garfunkel, and The Doors, as well as my love for hamburgers, hot dogs, and pretzels. I stood no chance; I had lost my heart to the American Dream. At the first opportunity, I bolted.

Without understanding what I was doing, I kept repeating my affirmation of orders to my subconscious mind as a way to develop the emotion of faith. Years later, I realized what I had been doing. In the chapter on "Faith" in *Think and Grow Rich*, Napoleon Hill explains:

> "Perhaps the meaning may be made clearer through the following explanation as to the way that men sometimes become criminals. Stated in the words of a famous criminologist, 'When men first come into contact with crime, they abhor it. If they remain in contact with crime for a time, they become accustomed to it, and endure it. If they remain in contact with it long enough, they finally embrace it, and become influenced by it.'"

The process is the same with faith; if you remain in contact with it long enough, you finally embrace it. Any impulse or thought that is repeatedly passed on to the subconscious mind is, finally, accepted and acted upon by the subconscious mind, which proceeds to translate that impulse into its physical equivalent. This is because all thoughts that have been emotionalized (given feeling), and mixed with faith, begin immediately to translate themselves into their physical equivalent or counterpart.

The proof is simple and easily shown. It is wrapped up in the principle of auto-suggestion. It is a well-known fact that one comes, finally, to believe whatever one repeats to one's self, whether the statement is true or false. If a person repeats a lie over and over, that person will eventually accept the lie as truth. That is why the statement, "Fake it till you make it" is such an effective strategy.

Each person is what he or she is because of the dominating thoughts that they permit to occupy their minds: thoughts that a person deliberately places in his mind and emotionalizes create the motivating forces which direct and control his every movement, act, and deed. Hill concludes that, "A thought thus 'magnetized' with emotion may be compared to a seed which, when planted in fertile soil, geminates, grows, and multiplies itself, over and over again, until that which was originally one small seed becomes countless millions of seeds."

In retrospect, one small seed, a thought magnetized with emotion, was a decision I made after meeting my psychiatrist back around 1980. That seed was the right decision for me. I know this because rarely do we make decisions without a cost, without an injury, and often to all parties involved, and Stephan Hoeller captures the idea when he said, "Pearls are beautiful things that are produced by an injured life, and if we have not been injured, then we will not produce the pearl." This painful time was a healing crisis. We are letting go of something old so that we can open up to something new. We must allow ourselves to feel the fear and sadness and remind ourselves that there is a gift we simply can't see yet. I often think of many old friends from my youth, and I am grateful not only for their love and friendship but also for their challenges, because I now see them as gifts or blessings in disguise.

3
DESIRE

"Desire is the most powerful instrument."
Napoleon Hill

The Woman of My Dreams

In April 1980, I was invited to the birthday party of
Suzanne – a childhood friend – held at the *Villa de Cesare*,
a now-vanished Italian restaurant on the Embankment in
London. There, I met a chestnut-haired woman with almond-
shaped eyes, who went by the name of Talyn. I had seen
her only twice before: once when she was six years old in
the Sudan and then at age sixteen at her uncle's home in
Wimbledon. That night, after dinner, the band started
playing *That's the Way I Like It* by KC and the Sunshine Band.
Pumped up with rhythm, I jived over to Talyn's table and
asked her to dance. She accepted, and we danced for what felt
like too short a time. I felt drawn to her, comfortable in my
skin, and I liked her; but she did not let on that she liked me.
I was left confused and wondering what that was all about.

I did not see her again for another two years. Then, out of
the blue, Talyn's brother, Krikor, contacted me, and we started

jogging twice a week, after work. Soon, on the weekends, we were on two-mile runs, and a few months later, we ended up doing an eight-mile run from Westminster to Wimbledon. On reaching Wimbledon, their mother offered me tea and biscuits, and before I left to go home, they invited me out to dinner that evening at San Lorenzo, a local restaurant.

I arrived at the restaurant at 7:30 and was ushered to their table, where I saw that Talyn had also come along. I like to think that she had been impressed by the fact that I had run eight miles. Perhaps she may even have thought I had run for her. We still occasionally debate what actually happened that evening. After that, her brother and I had planned to go to Tokyo Joe's, a club in Piccadilly. I asked her if she wanted to join us, and she accepted. At the bar in the club, waiting for our drinks, I sensed from our body language and conversation that we had a connection: something had clicked between us. After that evening, we started dating, and in April 1983, we were engaged. A few months later, Talyn, who was a graduate of Camberwell School of Art with a first class degree in Sculpture, received a letter notifying her that she had won a scholarship to study Art in Rome for two years. To this day, I am surprised that she declined it to marry me. On September 9th that year, we were married in London at St. Peter's Church in Cranley Gardens.

Living in America

As I said previously, I was enamored with America. I had spent several summers traveling through the US, including New York, New Jersey, Arizona, and California, and I had fallen in love with the majestic beauty of the landscape, the open and warm spirit of the American people, and their indomitable faith in the growth and progress of humanity. So, when the opportunity came to live and work in the US, I grabbed it with both hands.

In May 1985, Talyn and I moved to New Jersey. Initially, we stayed with my brother Chris, who had rented a house near Princeton, in central New Jersey, for a few months, because my parents had invested in an office property there since 1980. However, so we could be near New York City for work, we moved to North Jersey and settled in Ridgewood, a picturesque town, which became home for us. Our two daughters were born in Ridgewood's Valley Hospital.

Before moving to the US, Chris and I had made arrangements with a British leather upholstery company to be appointed as their representatives in the US. We chose this manufacturer because they were commissioned to re-upholster the tufted leather seats in both Houses of Parliament, and we knew that Americans would love to own sofas and armchairs that had this historic cachet, so we came out with the slogan: "Our act has been passed by Parliament." We opened an office in Hackensack to start Ibis Furniture, Inc., and we enlisted a number of showrooms and galleries in design centers across the US to display and sell our products to designers and architects. We operated with moderate success for two years. However, I had not gone to the US to seek moderate success.

In mid-1987, an opportunity presented itself. My parents were in trouble with their commercial property investment near Princeton. The property management agent was the former owner, who had given his guarantee to the two mortgages on the property. He was now calling for my parents to invest significant monies to refurbish the property, which he was going to undertake as the contractor. My parents did not want to invest more, yet they could not fire the property management agent without triggering the payoff of the mortgages. They were cornered.

Chris and I volunteered to sort it out. My knowledge of Napoleon's war tactics, which was harvested from the late Brian Keelan, one of the smartest boys in my year at Douai

School, proved most useful. This was a war I welcomed, and I worked it as though I had already won it. We approached our lawyers in Hackensack, and through them, we were introduced to a leading local bank, which, after due diligence on the said property, offered to give us one mortgage to pay off the existing two. We then interviewed several property management agents and selected one, who after thirty-five years is still working with us. We also appointed new accountants and new insurance brokers. On April 3, 1987, on my father's sixty-seventh birthday, we sent three motorcycle couriers to fire the former property management agent, the former lawyer, the former accountant, the former insurance broker, and the former two banks that held the mortgages. We performed these actions with military precision, along the lines that Emperor Napoleon would have been proud. Once we had accomplished that, we sent my father a Western Union telegram and wrote: *Dearest Dad, Wishing you an amazing birthday Stop The coup was a success Stop Congratulations! Stop George and Chris.*

Why Is DESIRE Important?

Desire is important because it is the first step in renewing the mind. Desire is also the starting point of all achievement.

For much of my early life, I can honestly say that I did not know what my desire was. Nobody had sat me down and spoken to me, heart-to-heart. When I was eleven, I recall wanting to be a priest, but by sixteen, that desire fell by the wayside when I began to be attracted to girls. I enjoyed entertaining my family and friends with stories, and seeing them explode with laughter when I mimicked people. Given that I was a lover of films, I thought, for a time, of being an actor or a comedian, but that too fell away when I discovered that it was a financially precarious profession. After that, I was attracted to wealth and fame. I did often think and even professed that I would be a millionaire so that I could enjoy beautiful things, like houses, cars, clothes, and holidays but also so I could help people in need and fund worthy causes.

My favorite television program in my adolescence was *The Persuaders*, starring Roger Moore, playing an English aristocrat who drove an Aston Martin, Tony Curtis, playing a wealthy American with a Ferrari, and a retired judge, played by Laurence Naismith. Moore and Curtis would solve cases, brought to them by the retired judge, that the courts and the police were unable to solve. My close friend Robert Clifford-Holmes felt a resonance with Moore's character as I did for Curtis' (given my love for all things American). What made this series even more personal for us is that the late Laurence Naismith was the owner operator of the best country pub in our area – The Row Barge, which exists to this day and which I visited as recently as July 2017, with friends from Florida that I had not seen in over forty years.

All transformation begins with an intense, burning desire to be transformed. The first step in renewing of the mind is desire. Influential author and teacher, Neville Goddard, in his book *The Power of Awareness*, wrote this about desire:

> "You must make your future dream a present fact. You do this by assuming the feeling of your wish fulfilled. By desiring to be other than what you are, you can create an ideal of the person you want to be and assume that you are already that person. If this assumption is persisted in until it becomes your dominant feeling, the attainment of your ideal is inevitable…You must be like a moth in search of his idol, the flame…Just as the moth in his desire to know the flame was willing to destroy himself, so must you in becoming a new person be willing to die to your present self."

Our imagination is the instrument, the means, by which we create our new world. Imagination is the only redemptive power in the Universe.

Let us remember that Columbus dreamed of an unknown world, staked his life on the existence of such a world, and discovered it. Copernicus, the great astronomer, dreamed of a multiplicity of worlds and revealed them. Henry Ford dreamed of a horseless carriage, went to work, and his dream is now seen the world over. Thomas Edison dreamed of a lamp that could be operated by electricity, and despite ten thousand failures, he stood by his dream until he made it a physical reality. The Wright brothers dreamed of a machine that would fly through the air, and now the evidence is everywhere. Beethoven was deaf, Milton was blind, but their names will last as long as time endures, because they translated their dreams into organized thought. Jeff Bezos dreamed of an online bookshop, and now Amazon is the world's biggest bookstore, grocery store, and so much more.

Any great achievement is, at first and for a time, but a dream. Just as the oak sleeps in the acorn, or the bird waits in the egg, dreams are the seedlings of reality. The turning point in the lives of those who succeed usually comes at the moment of some crisis, through which they are introduced to their 'other selves.' It's interesting and telling to note that this is confirmed in the Chinese culture, where the characters for "crisis" and "opportunity" are the same.

Thomas Troward could not stress enough that "desire" is paramount. Desire is the force behind all things; it is the principle action of the Universe and the innermost center of all life. Desire is the creative power, and it must be carefully guarded, trained, and directed.

"The desire and its fulfillment are bound together as cause and effect; and when we realize the law of their sequence, we shall be more than ever impressed with the supreme importance of Desire as the great center of Life."

By mid-1988, once we had put the commercial property back on track, Chris and I decided to close the furniture business. By then, I had also lost all interest in property management. For weeks, I felt so despondent I did not want to rise from my bed. All desire to continue in the property business had abandoned me as I saw no challenges in staying on. After several months, I finally reached an agreement with Chris that I would retain my shares in the business but resign from the active management of the business and allow him to run it.

This opened up an opportunity for me to search and seek what I most desired to do next. Even though I had no idea whatsoever what that might be, I knew it was the right thing to do, and I was excited about this new adventure, but I was also fearful.

4
THINKING

"Thinking is the hardest work there is."
Henry Ford

Same Vocation, New Paths

Sometime in 1990, after a Myers-Briggs personality test, and a full-day visit to the Johnson O'Connor Research Foundation in New York for tests and interviews, I discovered I was in the top 1% in the US for my communications skills. I had discovered my talent, and I wanted to use it in the most proficient manner. I was thirty-five years old then, and I did not want to waste another day. So, I proceeded to look into how to apply for Journalism school. I was compelled to go back to night school to study for the test required by these schools, which was the Graduate Record of Examination (GRE) before I could apply to local universities. This meant having to work out algebraic and quadratic equations, which I had not done for over seventeen years, and truth be told, I did not remember how to do them. Thankfully, after three months of training at Kaplan's in the evenings, I passed the

GRE test with an acceptable score. Ultimately, one morning, I received a letter from New York University informing me that they had accepted me to study for a Master's degree in Journalism.

I embarked on this journey with a sense of excitement and terror. I was excited about my new adventure of learning a new craft, for which it seemed I was destined. I was in a state of terror, because I would not have any income for the next eighteen months, so I was drawing on my savings, and I had an extra mouth to feed: a year earlier, in April 1989, Talyn gave birth to a baby girl, whom we named Victoria, a most precious gift.

My upbringing and education had taught me that "thinking people" or "thoughtful persons" take calculated risks, and that meant minimal risks. Why? Because intelligent people know that those who take big risks end up losing all they have. So, why would anyone intelligent do something stupid or illogical like that? Before embarking on this path, I considered myself smart because I lived within that mind-set. Unknowingly, I was pushing against the parameters of my old thinking. This was causing me some discomfort, which I began to live with and accept. Occasionally, there were times when traveling late in New York's subways on winter nights, exchanging the warm, urine-smelling, recycled air of the subways with the cold, blustery winds blowing down Manhattan avenues, that I wished I was in a more secure job, with a more pleasant lifestyle, but that feeling evaporated as soon as I wrote an engaging story.

What I was doing, unknowingly, was "thinking" outside the box. I was trusting my intuition, because I had seen the limitations of my conscious mind, which relied essentially on my limited five senses – seeing, hearing, smelling, touching, and tasting. My education had never taught me to trust my intuition. In fact, I can declare that intuition was considered close, perhaps even synonymous, to superstition. Yet, at all critical times in my life, I have trusted my intuition, and I have rarely gone wrong. In earlier days, I would have been reluctant to admit this fact openly for fear of being seen as a simpleton.

Our thoughts possess creative powers, but because we have used these in the wrong direction, they have produced limitations of which we complain, much like my past thinking that taking risks was unintelligent. All life is a risk, and security is an illusion. When we refuse to take any risk, we are not living: we are stunted. The greatest risk in life is to take no risk at all.

We are in charge of ourselves. As success coach and author Bob Proctor states:

"We cannot allow what is going on outside of us to control us. We have in our possession six tools or intellectual factors, which used properly will help us to create the kind of world that we desire, and they are: Perception, Will, Imagination, Memory, Reason, and Intuition. We generally live from the outside in, using our sensory factors – see, hear, smell, touch, and taste – because that is how we have been programed from childhood. We will never do anything of any consequence, as long as we live that way."

Let's look at a few of these intellectual factors. **Reason.** Most people know what they have to do to get the results they need, but they avoid taking action, because they don't like doing what they must. If we don't like the results we are getting, let's not allow the results to control our future. Think for a moment about your school report; let's say you received poor results in mathematics. We allow the poor mathematics result to register in our mind. Then the results cause us to

think we are useless at this subject. This thinking causes our bad **feelings** toward the subject, which provokes our **actions** in the following tests to continue to be poor, which produces more of the same result. This situation need not continue. We can and must change this vicious cycle by not allowing what is going on outside to control our minds.

J B Rhine, the American botanist and parapsychologist, wrote, "The mind is the greatest power in all creation." What Rhine means is not blasphemy but quite the contrary. What he means is that in all of God's creation, the mind is the greatest power, and he is so right.

Change your mind-set. Instead of thinking of the results you have now, think of the results you want. Build the image of the results you want in your mind. Then the thoughts cause the feelings, the feelings cause the action, and the action causes the new results.

Why is it that we often see highly-educated people, who have graduated from the top universities, such as Harvard, Stanford, Oxford, and Cambridge, who have failed to achieve any success in life? Also, why is it that we often see people who have very little schooling achieve success far beyond the imagination of the wealthiest and most powerful people?

The answer is provided by Napoleon Hill:

"An educated person is not necessarily a person with an abundance of general or specialized knowledge. An educated person is someone who has so developed the faculties of their mind that they can acquire anything that they want or its equivalent without violating the rights of others."

Now let's look at **Perception**. There are many ways of looking at everything. If we see something and think it can't be done, we can change our point of view. Perhaps through a change in point of view, we'll find our answer. Wayne Dyer once said: "If we change the way we look at things, the things we look at change."

How about **Intuition**? This is a form of perception, but it is beyond the physical senses. It is that sensory system which operates without data from the five senses. Intuition serves survival. It prompts you to pursue that which has no apparent reason in order to survive. Intuition serves creativity, and it serves inspiration. There is a quote, whose source is unknown, but it speaks to the heart of the matter: "When we pray, we're talking to God; when we use our intuition, God is talking to us."

As we are made in the image of God, we too have creative powers, and as Thomas Troward wrote:

"…The reason for the creative power of our thought is because our mind is itself a thought of the Divine mind and that consequently our increase in livingness and creative power must be in exact proportion to our perception of our relation to the Parent Mind."

This idea is not new. The idea that we are co-creators with God is an old Christian ideal, which is reinforced by the idea that we are all co-heirs of the Kingdom and as such, we are all sons and daughters of God. The lesson in the parable of the Prodigal Son clearly illustrates that being of divine origin, we can never really be separated from God or "the Parent Mind," which continually seeks expression through us.

Our thoughts have divine resonance, and we become what we think about. In his book *The Strangest Secret*, Earl Nightingale wrote:

"Throughout history, the great wise men and teachers, philosophers and prophets have disagreed with one another on many different things. It is only on this one point that they are in complete and unanimous agreement – the key to success and the key to failure is this: We become what we think about."

Let me repeat: **We become what we think about**.

Earl Nightingale was not exaggerating. Several people before him also said it.

The illustrious Roman Emperor Marcus Aurelius said: "A man's life is what his thoughts make of it." Ralph Waldo Emerson wrote: "A man is what he thinks about all day long." Lastly, William James said: "The greatest discovery of my generation is that human beings can alter their lives by altering their attitudes of mind."

By altering their attitudes of mind, William James is talking about faith and belief, brought about by one's way of thinking. "All things are possible to him who believes," (Mark 9-23). This is not new thinking; Jesus also clearly understood what manifestation was all about, when he said, "So I tell you, whatever you ask for in prayer, believe that you have received it, and it will be yours." (Mark 11:24)

There's more to this story. Many Christians might not agree with my interpretations of this next passage in the Bible, but it is so clear, I can't see how it can be misconstrued:

"In all truth I tell you, whoever believes in me will perform the same works as I do myself, and will perform even greater works." (John 14:12)

This is an astonishing and remarkable statement. Allow your mind to dwell upon this for a few minutes. What Jesus was saying is that we can perform the same miracles as he did, and even greater one. So why can't we? I suspect it is because we don't believe we can. What if we believed? Now, that's a frightening prospect, isn't it?

A few years ago, I came across a quote by Marianne Williamson, American author and spiritual teacher, in which she said, "Our deepest fear is not that we are inadequate. Our deepest fear is that we are powerful beyond measure. It is our Light, not our Darkness, that most frightens us." I am certain that we are afraid of our light, our power. I thought that was an amazing concept at the time, but I did not really understand it until recently. Williamson reaffirms what Jesus was saying over 2,000 years ago, and for some reason or another, this clear declaration was lost until now. Or is it perhaps only because the time is now opportune, we can understand what this means for us today?

It's clear as day that if a person is thinking about a concrete goal, they will reach it, because that's what they are thinking about. And we become what we think about. Conversely, if a person has no goal and doesn't know where they are going, their thoughts will be confusion, anxiety, fear, and worry, and they become what they think about, which is reflected in the unhappiness of their life.

People are always blaming their circumstances for what they are bringing to fruition. George Bernard Shaw believed that "The people that get on in this world are the people who get up and look for the circumstances they want and, if they can't find them, make them."

This well-known adage, "As you sow, so shall you reap," applies to the soil as much as it does to your subconscious mind. Whatever you plant in the soil is what you will reap. If you plant corn, you will reap corn; if you plant deadly nightshade, a poison, that is what you will reap. Plant positive thoughts into your subconscious mind so that you reap positive results.

You Become What You Think About.

I became what I thought about – a Journalist. I worked for three months as an intern at CNBC television station, in Fort Lee, New Jersey, and while I was there, I worked on a documentary project called *Kiwi Airlines*, using quality video footage from the CNBC Library, which helped me to attain a College Emmy Award the following year. In April 1993, a month before I graduated, we had the gift of a second daughter, whom we named Elizabeth. Early that year, Talyn and I had decided that after I graduated from NYU, we would return to London to start a new episode in our lives.

In May 1993, we moved to London. I sought work at CNBC and various other news organizations and found no serious employment. After six months, I started to look outside the media world. I found an opportunity to work as a self-employed financial advisor at Allied Dunbar PLC, a life insurance company, for three years, and thereafter as an independent financial advisor for two years. Then, in 1999, on a winter holiday in Switzerland, I met an Internet guru, and on discerning that we had synergies, we decided to write books together for his educational and networking organization.

5
CREATIVITY

"Creativity is the Hidden Power."
Thomas Troward

Obstacles Are the Way

After a five-year hiatus from writing, I was back to writing books, and I loved it.

From 1999 to 2002, I collaborated with Thomas Power, an Internet guru, and wrote three books with and for him. The first was *Battle of the Portals* (1999), a visionary book about how the Internet would create new economic and social portals. It was self-published and created a lot of noise. The second book was *Ecosystem: The 12 Principles of e-Business* (2001), which was published by the Financial Times/Pearson Education and took two years to produce, because it took a great deal of time to interview over fifty people for their views. The third book was *Xerox Firestorm* (2002), which was commissioned and paid for by Xerox but was never published, for internal reasons that I am legally precluded from disclosing.

By 2002, in the aftermath of the Internet bubble and the 9/11 attacks on the Twin Towers in New York City, which caused economic activity to slow to a standstill, I decided to move on, and to focus on writing a personal story, to pull away from all the negative distraction around me. On reflection, I now understand the wisdom of the adage, "Obstacles are the way." Were it not for this obstacle, the chances of my finding time to write these books were infinitesimal. This story – *The Truth Will Set Us Free: Armenians and Turks Reconciled* (2003) – was my maternal grandmother's story of exile and loss, genocide and trauma, and I used it for a higher purpose: to dovetail truth with reconciliation between these two peoples. I went on a five-city book tour of the United States to deliver talks on my book to the Armenian communities. My ideas were generally well received, except by the highly concentrated Armenian community in Glendale, Los Angeles, who were politely hostile to my way of thinking. My book was translated into Turkish, and my publisher faced several public prosecutions for publication, because by publishing it he had contravened Article 301 of the Turkish penal code, which makes reference to insulting the Turkish nation. I am reliably informed that this is one way that the Turkish authorities stifle free speech.

In 2004, following my father's death, I was moved to write a book on his ancestral hometown in Ottoman Turkey: *Arabkir: Homage to an Armenian Community*. The original work in Armenian was published in New York in 1969 and was over 1,000 pages long and had some fifty contributing editors. It was to all intents and purposes unread. With a financial contribution from my mother, I had the book translated into English and wrote a one hundred and fifty page abridged version. Although I completed the manuscript that same year, it was not published for another decade.

In 2006, I was commissioned by two Bahamas residents to write a biography of their father, an Armenian exile from

Ottoman Turkey, who had made good in Anglo-Egyptian Sudan. A limited edition of this book, *Sarkis Izmirlian; A Biography*, was published in 2008 for their family members only and is not available for sale.

Between 2007 and 2011, in my spare time, I wrote a lengthy and graphic novel on a legal case, but my lawyers advised me not to have it published, because of potential libel, as those close to the matter might be able to claim that identities would be obvious to those linked to the subject, and then they would be able to claim damages. I decided to withhold the publication indefinitely.

In the fall of 2012, I went on a pilgrimage to the Holy Land (Israel) with a dozen pilgrims, which had a profound effect on me. I took prolific notes, and acting as a witness, I wrote a book called *Seeking God: A Pilgrimage in the Holy Land*, which was published in 2013.

The reason I chose this quote, "Obstacles are the way," is because if obstacles had not been put in my life, I would not have had the time and the opportunity to write the books that I did, most specifically, my personal stories, stories of my family, and the troubled history of the Armenian people. It is the obstacles in my life that helped me to take this journey less traveled, and for this, I am most grateful.

Using selected paragraphs from the works of three writers, Thomas Troward, Neville Goddard, and Earl Nightingale, I try to answer the following three questions: How do we acquire the hidden power of creativity? Why is it available to all of us to use? And lastly, how does a creative person think and act?

How Do We Acquire the Hidden Power of Creativity?

In his book, *The Hidden Power* (1921), Thomas Troward, explains how we all have access to the hidden power of creativity. He wrote, "The I AM in the individual is none other than the I AM in the universal." The I AM who I am, or Yahweh, is taken from the Book of Exodus in the Bible. What Troward means is that we humans are made in the image of God, and so we are, in essence, so much more powerful that we give ourselves credit. Hence, we are also children of God, heirs to His Kingdom, and His co-creators on earth. He adds that because of our spiritual nature, the power is inherent in us, and it is our marvelous heritage. If not intelligently and constructively used, this power will express its uncontrolled force with devastating energy. "If it is not used to build up, it will destroy."

The power of suggestion is a hidden power, but the power that creates all things is the hidden power, which is at the back of all things.

We all have the hidden power of creativity, but we are programmed from infancy with limitations. "Limitations surround us because we believe in our inability to do what we desire. Whenever we say, 'I cannot,' we cease to exercise our thought-power in that direction because we believe ourselves stopped by a blank wall of impossibility; and whenever this occurs we are subjected to bondage," writes Thomas Troward.

"Our lives are part of the Universal Source, just as much as a glass of seawater is part of the vast oceans. If it were not, where does it come from? Jesus revealed this great truth to the Samaritan woman when he spoke of it as a spring of Life, forever welling up within us. Again, to the multitude assembled at the Temple, he spoke of it as a river of life, forever gushing from the secret sources of the spirit within us. Life to be ours at all must be within us. So, Jesus does not direct us to an external source of Life, but reveals to us that the Kingdom of Heaven is internal; it is within us. The creative power is within us because we are made in the image of God, and so we have access to infinite power, if only we can believe in it."

Why Is It Available to All of Us to Use?

In *The Power of Awareness* (1952), Neville Goddard shared a concept about creation that initially surprised me. Then it opened the eyes of my mind to the power of awareness. After reading it a few times and contemplating it, it makes complete sense. Not only does it not conflict with the book of Genesis, but in fact, it affirms it. He writes, "Creation is finished." In other words, all that we have ever been or ever will be exists now. Everything has already been created, some have already manifested, and the rest is yet to be manifested.

The fact that you can never be anything that you are not already or experience anything not already existing explains the experience of having an acute feeling of having heard before what is being said, having met a new person before, or having seen a place or thing that you are seeing for the first time.

As Neville Goddard said in *The Power of Awareness*:

"If creation is finished, and all events are taking place now, the question that springs to mind is – what determines your time track?... the answer is – your concept of yourself. For example, if you assume that you have a wonderful business, you will notice how *in your imagination* your attention is focused on incident after incident relating to that assumption. Persistence in this assumption will result in actually experiencing in fact that which you assumed."

Therefore, if you believe in what you are doing, you can conceive and achieve it.

How Does a Creative Person Think and Act?

In his spoken word recordings, *The Strangest Secret*, (1957), Earl Nightingale gives his definition. "The creative person realizes that his mind is an inexhaustible storehouse. He will have a clearly defined set of goals toward which he is working. The creative person knows his brain thrives on exercise. He reaches out for ideas.

"As ideas are like slippery fish, creative persons must always have a pad and a pencil handy so that they can capture ideas immediately and not risk forgetting them. As creative persons are intensely observant, they must absorb everything they see and hear. They should also believe that any person they meet must be the most important person in that room and give them their full, undivided attention.

"The creative person anticipates achievement. He expects to win. He knows it is a waste of time merely to worry about problems, so he wisely invests the same time and energy in solving problems. The creative person knows the value of giving himself and his ideas away."

And so it is for me, as a creative person, that I have given myself away as well as my ideas. For me, writing brings order out of chaos, and to do so means wading into the chaos, which I enjoy, because there is a sense of adventure, challenge, and joy. I have often resorted to writing, when I have faced difficult times in my life, as a way to channel my stress into something creative and not destructive. Writing is power, because it is about new ideas, and new ideas influence and change people, for better or worse. Yet this creative power is also a hidden power, because on the surface few understand where it comes from. Even writers struggle with what is loosely termed "writer's block." This means they have no inspiration, because they have blocked it by trying to control the process instead of allowing it to flow. Inspiration or "breathing in" is the operative word, because without it, there is no creativity. So, where does this inspiration come from? In my understanding, it comes from the Universal Spirit, or the Holy Spirit, or I AM, because we are made in the image of God, so when we hook up to this Universal Spirit, all manner of creativity flows through us.

In 2014, on the eve of the centenary of the Armenian Genocide (1915-2015), I finally decided to publish *Arabkir: Homage to an Armenian Community*. In 2003, just before my father's death, I had discovered a steel Chubb box in a cupboard in my parents' London apartment. This steel box contained one hundred glass-plate photographs, which my mother informed me were taken by my paternal grandfather of his hometown of Arabkir and his college town of Erzerum. Over the following decade, I tried to loan these to a new Armenian-American Museum, in Washington DC, which was in the process of emerging but was still born. Thus, I decided to write a book and produce a thirty-minute documentary film titled *Daylight After a Century*. My family donated these 100 glass plates, the camera, and personal documentation and family photographs to the Armenian Genocide Museum in Yerevan, Armenia. In November 2015, along with my wife and two daughters, I visited Armenia for the first time, when an exhibition of these photographs opened at the museum, and I had the honor to be asked to deliver the opening speech.

6

GRATITUDE

"Thank you is the most important prayer."
Meister Eckhart

Perfect Storm of 2007

In December 2006, Talyn and I exchanged contracts with a buyer to sell our home in London, with completion and handover in February 2007, when we moved to a nearby apartment. In the middle of this process, in early January, we received a phone call from Krikor, Talyn's brother, to say that their father, who was living in Geneva, Switzerland, had suffered a stroke and was in a hospital. We flew out the next day, and we were there when he died a few days later. We returned a fortnight later to attend his funeral.

On our return to London after the funeral, I was scheduled for an MRI on my colon. After the MRI, I was waiting in the reception, and the nurse came in and asked me if I was complaining about a growth on my pelvis. I said no, and at first I thought that she had the wrong patient. It then occurred to me that they might have found something sinister. The nurse came out and told me that she had arranged for a follow-up appointment at 10 am the next day with my consultant. I knew something was wrong, but I was left hanging.

The following morning at 10 am, I arrived at the consultant's offices, with my wife and my brother Jack, who is a doctor. The consultant told us that my colon was fine, but that the MRI had revealed a large tumor, the size of an eggplant, which was sitting on my pelvis. The consultant had taken the liberty to arrange an appointment with an oncologist an hour later in the same medical center.

The oncologist confirmed the finding, and he said that because bone tumors were invariably secondary cancers, this meant that the cancer would have spread around the whole body. Then he dropped the bombshell: "In 98% of bone tumor cases, the prospects are dim – perhaps six more months of life." However, he said he would need to do various tests over the next few weeks to confirm his diagnosis. Talyn and I went home shell-shocked.

Over the next few weeks, while these tests were ongoing, I discovered to my surprise that I was not afraid of death, but I was anxious about the future welfare of my daughters, who would not have their father to turn to in times of crisis. Each morning on rising, I would seek the sunrise, and when I saw it, I would wonder how many of them I would see before my impending departure.

While undergoing medical tests and waiting for the results, Talyn and I spent those three weeks finishing the frenetic packing in the home that we had sold and ensuring that all the boxes were properly marked to go to our new rental apartment or to a storage warehouse in Battersea. When we reflect on this time, we still wonder how we actually managed to do the work; it seemed as though we were in a hazy trance. We moved into our rental apartment in early February, and by the end of the month, we were just about settled.

In early March, the full medical results were in, and we went to see the oncologist, who informed us that he had some good news and some bad news. The good news was that the tumor was thankfully benign, meaning there was no presence of malignant cancer. I belonged to the lucky 2% club. The bad news was that because the tumor was so large, it had to be removed by surgery, and convalescence would take up to six months. To me this felt like my death sentence had been commuted to six months imprisonment. I jumped for joy and punched the air with my right fist.

The following day, we were passed on to see a surgeon, a genial young man in his thirties, who informed me, with a smile, that he would cut the side of my right leg in the shape of the Mercedes Benz star, because he said, "You are worth it!" I pointed out to him that he was mixing advertising metaphors, but he just chuckled. In early April, the first operation was three hours long and required him to block the arteries to the tumor. The second operation, a week later, lasted five hours, in which he removed the tumor, in three separate pieces. Following the operation, I was in intensive care for the first two days, and the nights seemed as if I were in Dante's Inferno, where I was half asleep, hearing others moaning and groaning all night in their pain. It was relative bliss to move to a private ward for the next five days. Unable to wash myself, I was grateful for the wonderful Zimbabwean nurse, who helped to wash me every day. It was so good to come home to my family and to the warmth and comfort of my own bed.

Bizarre as it may sound, I am most grateful for my close encounter with death. Sometimes, the greatest cause for gratitude lies concealed in the challenges we face, for they help to make us stronger and more compassionate. The bone tumor that appeared in my body was not the curse I thought it was; it was a gift. This "gift" of a bone tumor would become my wakeup call. I would see the rest of my life as a "gift" or bonus. I now see everything as a gift from the Universe, and what I make of this life is my gift back to it. When confronted with our mortality, we learn how limited our time is here on earth, and it intensifies our awareness of what a treasure life is. Even though I am an extrovert and love meeting new people, I now spend more time with the people I love. I know my priorities.

Gratitude is a palpable substance radiating from the person experiencing this emotion, and this substance radiates and inspires the people who come into contact with it. It seems so counter-intuitive and counter-cultural, but I am so grateful for this bone tumor. My life has been enriched immensely because of it, and each new day is alive with new possibilities that I can experience.

In our preoccupation with what isn't there, we miss what is here. Gratitude is not the result of things that happen to us; it is an attitude we cultivate, and the first step is to appreciate the love we already have. There is so much depth to gratitude that the mystic Meister Eckhart said that "Thank You" is the most important prayer, and the poet William Blake said, "Gratitude is Heaven itself."

"Whole-hearted thanksgiving engages the whole person," writes Brother David Steindl-Rast. "The intellect recognizes the gift as gift. Thanksgiving presupposes thinking. The will, in its turn, acknowledges the interdependence of the giver and thanks-giver. And the emotions celebrate the joy of that mutual belonging. Only when intellect, will and emotions join together does thanksgiving become genuine, whole-hearted."

"Gratitude is a powerful process of shifting our energy and bringing more of what we want in our lives," wrote Rhonda Byrne of *The Secret*. "Be grateful for what you already have and you will attract more good things."

In his book *The Science of Getting Rich* (1910), Wallace D Wattles, wrote a whole chapter on gratitude and he boils it down to one sentence, "The whole process of mental adjustment can be summed up in one word: gratitude." In other words, no progress can be made in our mental growth whatsoever without first being in a state of gratitude, because gratitude puts us in a higher state of vibration, which is necessary for mental lift-off. Therefore, what Wattles is saying is that gratitude is the bedrock of happiness and success.

Many people, whose lives are mostly lived well, are kept in poverty by their lack of gratitude. It is easy to understand that the nearer we live to the source of wealth, the more wealth we shall receive. It is also easy to understand that a soul that is always grateful lives in closer touch with God, the Source, than one who never looks to Him in thankful acknowledgement.

We already possess good things because of certain laws, and this will keep us in close harmony with creative thought and prevent us from falling into competitive thought, where our focus moves to the gifts of others. If we focus and are grateful for our gifts and talents, this provides us with happiness, which prevents us from envy or jealousy of the gifts of others.

"The law of gratitude is the natural principle that action and reaction are always equal and in opposite directions," writes Wattles. "The grateful outreaching of your mind in thankful praise to the Supreme Power is a liberation or expenditure of force; it cannot fail to reach that to which it is addressed." Power cannot be exercised without gratitude, because it is gratitude that keeps you connected with power.

"Also, faith is born of gratitude. The grateful mind continually expects good things, and expectation becomes faith. The reaction of gratitude upon one's own mind produces faith. Every outgoing wave of grateful thanksgiving increases faith. The person who has no feeling of gratitude cannot long retain faith."

Every individual has a journey. We all try the best we can, and all of us fail, sometimes spectacularly, but that is the human condition. It is not our place to judge others. We should not rage against corrupt politicians, because if it were not for them, we would have anarchy, and our opportunities would be greatly diminished. We do not live in a perfect world, but the Source has a plan that is unfolding, and we should be grateful for our imperfect world. As Wattles writes, "This will bring you into a harmonious relationship with the good in everything, and the good in everything will move toward you."

Bob Proctor, author of *The ABCs of Success*, also wrote a chapter on gratitude, which states, "It is unfortunate but true that for many people, 'life' is something that is going to happen in the future. They are always looking forward to the arrival of that big event or that big day." In the anticipation of this event in the future, they miss out on the present.

More than forty scientific studies have shown that gratitude makes us feel happier, healthier, and wealthier, while providing us with more resilient personalities, more satisfying relationships, more fulfilling work, and strengthening our sense of community. The endless list of benefits was compiled by aggregating the results of these research studies on gratitude.

Robert Emmons, a professor of psychology for the past thirty years at the University of California, Berkeley, is the world's leading scientific expert on gratitude. He explains the benefits of gratitude: "First, gratitude allows celebration of the present, magnifying what you already have so as to extract more benefit from it. Second, gratitude blocks toxic emotions, such as envy, resentment, regret, and depression. Third, grateful people are more stress-resilient, and so recover far quicker from anxiety illness, and trauma. Fourth and last, gratitude strengthens social ties and self-worth."

In his book *Gratitude Works*, Emmons writes, "Since the time of the ancient philosopher Seneca, having an overly high opinion of one self has been seen as the chief obstacle to feeling and expressing gratitude. Research has shown that people who are ungrateful tend to have a sense of excessive self-importance, arrogance, vanity, and a high need for admiration and approval.

"For me to feel grateful for what I receive, I must translate my entitlements into gifts and recognize that we have no claim on them. If we are able to see these as given to us for our benefit without them being owed to us, we will be far less likely to develop an unhelpful attitude to entitlement. Eliminating entitlement from your life and embracing gratitude and humility are spiritually and psychologically liberating. Gratitude is the recognition that life owes me nothing at all and all the good I have is a gift."

This is a major shift in our mind-set. By moving away from a state of mind of "entitlement" to a state of mind of seeing life as a "gift," we change our focus toward a life of gratitude. This pivot to gratitude rewires our neural connections and synapses. As our thinking changes, so do our feelings and, as a result, our actions. These feelings of gratitude raise our vibrational frequency and make us feel happy and joyful. When we communicate with others, these feelings are transmitted. As our actions change, so do the reactions of people with whom we connect.

Generally, we take so many things for granted. Should we not be grateful for our health, minds, bodies, and spirits? Should we not be grateful for our spouses, partners, children, parents, and friends? Should we not be grateful for the roof over our heads? Should we not be grateful that we have running water and heating at home? That we have clothes, laptops, Internet, Wi-Fi, mobile phones, all kinds of transport, music, books, and civilization at our fingertips? We have so much to be grateful for. If we focus on what we don't have, we repel the very things we want. If we focus on the riches we already possess, we become happy and grateful, and we attract more of what we want.

At the core of the practice of gratitude is memory and remembering. In today's world, we have lost our sense of gratitude for the freedoms we enjoy, for the sacrifices others have made in the past for our freedoms, and for the material advantages we enjoy. Perhaps our consumer society and its relentless quest to create lifelong customers out of us has made us complacent and numbed our spirit of gratitude.

We humans are a paradox. We focus on the negative and dismiss the positive. Why else is the news media always focused on negative news? We rarely hear good news, because good news doesn't sell. Prof. Emmons provides an apt quote from neuroscientist Rick Hanson to explain this condition: "Our minds are Velcro for negative information but Teflon for positive." In other words, negative information sticks to us, while positive information glides off us.

One should not practice gratitude only when times are good. We should practice it even more when times are not good. Certainly, it is more difficult to practice when we are not feeling grateful, but the point is not about "feeling" grateful but about "thinking" grateful. By initiating our thinking, we engage our feeling to follow suit. One way to do so may be to imagine what the silver lining might be in any given situation. We can be grateful even if we do not feel it.

In his study of self-actualizers, (psychologist) Abraham Maslow, (who is best known for his "hierarchy of needs,") noted that "the most important learning experiences… were tragedies, deaths, and trauma… which forced change in the life-outlook of the person and consequently in everything that he did." As someone who has had a close encounter with death, I agree with this assertion completely. In fact, experiences of loss and disappointment can remove the superficial things in our lives that we cling to for meaning, allowing us to see the things of value that we had never before noticed.

In the words of Cicero, "Gratitude is not only the greatest of all the virtues, but the parent of all the others." The others virtues are humility, kindness, patience, diligence, charity, moderation, and abstinence. In our media-saturated society, our senses are stimulated toward the vices of pride, envy, wrath, sloth, greed, gluttony, and lust. Gratitude is the antidote to these vices. It cannot coexist with these vices. If you're in a grateful state, try and see if you can be envious. It's simply not possible. Gratitude blocks envy and all the other vices. Without the spirit of gratitude, our endeavors are temporary and fleeting. This is why I believe the spirit of gratitude is the key to our success, in whatever we choose to do.

It is all very well and good to have objectives and goals, but we must be mindful and consciously aware of the wonderful little events happening now in the present moment. The past is gone, the future is not ours to know; all we have is the "present" – a gift that we have been given, a gift that we must graciously receive, and open with joy and wonder. And if we are grateful even before we receive it, this is the stuff that creates miracles.

After the operation to remove my bone tumor, I lost a great deal of muscle and power in my legs; muscles that had taken years to burnish. Even my weight dropped by 10 kilos down to 78, a number I had not seen on any weighing machine since I was eighteen years old. My recuperation did take six months, with a fair amount of exercise each day and physical therapy each week. I took the opportunity to fill my days with studying a subject I had always wanted to learn: philosophy. I was grateful for the free time I now had to study.

When the student is ready, the teacher will appear. I purchased Prof. Daniel N Robinson's DVD course, The Great Ideas of Philosophy, and I spent the next few months watching his thirty-minute seminars, each and every morning, where I learned concepts from Aristotle to Wittgenstein. The timing could not have been more perfect to study this subject, and I enjoyed it immensely. Sometimes, the Universe, the Source, God, or whatever you prefer to call Him, throws us a curve ball to stop us in our tracks and question what we are doing. This is what He did to me, and for that I am eternally grateful.

7
DECISIONS

"One of the most important decisions you'll ever make is choosing the kind of Universe you exist in; is it helpful and supportive or hostile and unsupportive?"

Wayne Dyer

Making a Difficult Decision

In April 2007, during my recuperation from surgery, Krikor approached me to help him. He told me that he was the executor of his father's estate, and he explained the problem he faced. His family's small pharmaceutical business had gone into administration (The UK version of Chapter 11 in the US) in 2002 due to cash flow problems exacerbated by his ambitious foray into the Chinese market. However, the company was asset rich in its range of products. This was proved when a month earlier, in March 2007, the administrator managed to sell all the stable of products to an emerging pharmaceutical company at an excellent price; the cash proceeds were in the administrator's bank accounts. This was the good news. The bad news was that that same month, the Chinese distributor put in a substantial and fraudulent claim, which decimated the value of the surplus that the shareholders would have received.

Along with this fraudulent claim, the Chinese distributor threatened to sue the administrator if his claim was rejected. The administrator appeared to be caught in a vice. If he rejected the claim, he would have to defend his decision in court, but he could not use the monies in his account to defend the rights of the shareholders, because they were ring-fenced for the benefit of the creditors. If he accepted the claim, he would face a separate claim from the shareholders. Unable to do his job, the administrator stalled for several years. My brother-in-law needed funds to defend his position.

As a business proposition, I was convinced this was a poor one and far too risky for my appetite. However, given that my wife's family name was at stake, I could not very well brush it off without some consideration. So, I proceeded at a slow and judicious pace in order to assess the risks before making a commitment and in the hope that my wife might insist in stopping me. Thankfully, she didn't, so I proceeded. The legal advice I received was that if I decided to proceed, I had to be extremely careful not to put my head above the parapet, because of the financial consequences, if we lost our challenge. All my life, I had taken legal advice so as not to find myself in this position. God certainly has a sense of humor.

After signing an agreement with Krikor, I proceeded slowly and painfully like Odysseus after the end of the Trojan War. It took three grueling years of seeking and securing historical records of the company's activities, reading, digesting, and evaluating the material to see if we could create a plausible argument that an injustice had been done to the shareholders. Then in early 2010, we made a beachhead: we discovered quite by accident that one of the crucial documents, submitted by the Chinese distributor, was an undeniable forgery. We tried to negotiate from this position of strength, but our adversary refused.

In May 2010, we attended a hearing in the Royal Courts of Justice in London, which lasted five long days. Finally, we won a resounding victory, when our barrister proved conclusively that the Chinese distributor's claim was a forgery and had no merit. The documents he had produced were false, because the place name on the purported invoice was the name as it is known today, not what it was known as in 1998. The devil is in the detail. Lastly, our adversary also reimbursed me for my costs, almost in full, without any effort on my part to chase for it. In his written opinion in July of that same year, the judge wrote that our adversary was "a most unsatisfactory witness," commenting, "the sheer weight of the number and substance of the discrepancies in his evidence undermines his credibility" and concluded that our adversary "has shown himself to be dishonest in the fabrication of documents."

When we make a decision, it means we have chosen to go with one thing at the exclusion of all others. The word "decision" comes from the Latin word "*decisio*" meaning "cutting off." Often, decisions are not difficult, because we know what we want, and we have the facts at hand. The difficult decisions are the ones where we don't have all the facts, and we don't know what we want. In 2007, I faced such a decision.

The quandary was that, as an astute business person, I did not want to become involved in a matter of such high risk; however, I felt a compulsion to protect my wife's family assets and her family name. If I had made the decision to walk away, I would have saved myself a great deal of time, money, and effort, but I would have felt a lesser man. If I made the decision to become involved, which I did, I knew that it would cost me time, money, and effort, but in my gut, I knew that it was the right thing to do.

I also felt a strong pull to accept this challenge, for reasons I could not understand. Had God saved me from death by bone tumor so as to place this challenge before me? Perhaps if I had not had an aborted appointment with death, I may not have taken this challenge? Was the Universe throwing me an opulent opportunity disguised as a daunting difficulty? Whether a danger or an opportunity, I made the decision to take it. I entered into the spirit of it.

In his book *Think and Grow Rich* (1937), Napoleon Hill wrote, "Procrastination, the opposite of decision, is a common enemy, which practically every man must conquer."

Hill did not make this as a casual remark; his comments were based on twenty-five years of research. He stated that analysis (of interviews) of over 25,000 men and women, who had experienced failure, disclosed the fact that lack of decision was near the head of the list of the thirty major causes of failure. This was not a theory but a fact.

"Analysis of several hundred people who had accumulated fortunes well beyond the million dollar mark disclosed the fact that every one of them had the habit of reaching decisions promptly, and of changing these decisions slowly, if and when they were changed. People, who fail to accumulate money, without exception, have the habit of reaching decisions, if at all, very slowly, and of changing these decisions quickly and often."

The majority of people who fail to accumulate money sufficient for their needs are generally easily influenced by the opinions of others. Let's face it; opinions are the cheapest commodities on earth, and everyone has a flock of them ready to be wished on anyone willing to accept them. If you are influenced by the opinions of others, you will have no desire of your own.

Hill advises us to keep our own counsel when reaching our own decisions and take no one into our confidence, unless they are in our inner circle. Close friends and relatives, while not meaning to do so, often handicap us through their opinions and sometimes through ridicule, which is meant to be humorous. You have a brain and a mind of your own. Use it and reach your own conclusions. If you need facts or information from other people, to help you reach your decisions, acquire these quietly, without disclosing your purpose. Keep your eyes and ears wide open – and your mouth closed, if you wish to acquire the habit of prompt decision. Genuine wisdom is usually conspicuous through modesty and silence.

The greatest decision of all time, in Hill's view, was reached in Philadelphia on July 4, 1776, when fifty-six men signed their names to a document, which they well knew would bring freedom to all Americans or leave every one of the fifty-six hanging from the gallows.

While most people know the story and history of the American Revolution – my favorite topic – few realize the courage that decision required. Hill contends that when we read history of the Revolution, we falsely imagine that George Washington was the Father of the Country, while the truth is that Washington was an accessory after the fact. He states this not to rob Washington of the glory he richly merited but to give greater attention to the astounding power that was the real cause of his victory.

A brief review of the events that gave birth to this power started with an incident in Boston on March 5, 1770, when British soldiers patrolling the streets created resentment among the colonists, who hurled stones and abuse at them. The commanding officer gave orders to fix bayonets and charge. The result was death and injury of many. The incident aroused such resentment that the Provincial Assembly called a meeting for the purpose of taking definite action. Two members of the Assembly were John Hancock and Samuel Adams, who declared that a move must be made to eject all

British soldiers from Boston. Remember the decision of these two men called for faith and courage, because it was dangerous. Adams was appointed to call on Governor Hutchinson and demand the withdrawal of the British troops, and the request was granted. Few realize that important changes usually begin in the form of a definite decision in the minds of a few people. Hill contends that John Hancock, Samuel Adams, and Richard Henry Lee, of the Province of Virginia, were the real Fathers of the Country. Lee became an important factor in this story, because he and Samuel Adams communicated frequently by letter, sharing their fears and hopes of the welfare of the people of their provinces. From this practice, Adams conceived the idea that a mutual exchange of letters between the thirteen colonies might help bring about the coordination of effort so badly needed in resolving their problems. Two years later, Adams presented the idea to the Assembly and a Committee of Correspondence was organized.

The British were not oblivious to what was happening. The Crown appointed a new governor, Governor Gage, whose first act was to send a messenger, Col. Fenton, to call on Samuel Adams, to offer him new benefits provided he ceased his opposition to the government. If he were to continue, he could be sent to England for trial for treason. Adams had two choices. Clearly, Adams was forced to reach instantly a decision that could have cost his life. The majority of men would have found it difficult to reach such a decision and may have sent an evasive reply. Adams' reply was, "You may tell Governor Gage that I trust I have long since made my peace with the King of Kings. No personal consideration shall induce me to abandon the righteous cause of my country... and tell Governor Gage it is the advice of Samuel Adams to him, no longer to insult the feelings of an exasperated people."

Governor Gage flew into a rage and issued a proclamation to pardon all those who lay down their arms but not Adams and Hancock. The governor's threat forced these two men to reach another decision, equally dangerous. They hurriedly called a secret meeting of their staunchest followers, and in that meeting, Adams declared that it was imperative to organize a Congress of the Colonists. A decision that day called for arrangements to be made for a meeting of the First Continental Congress to be held in Philadelphia on September 5, 1774. Hill contends that this date is more important than July 4, 1776, because if there had been no decision to hold a Continental Congress, there would have been no signing of the Declaration of Independence.

Hill concludes this story:

"It was such men as these who, without power, without authority, without military strength, without money, sat in solemn consideration of the destiny of the colonies, beginning at the opening of the First Continental Congress and continuing at intervals for two years until on June 7, 1776, Richard Henry Lee addressed the Chair and Assembly with this motion that 'these United Colonies be absolved from all allegiance to the Crown and that all political connection between them and the state of Great Britain is, and ought to be, totally dissolved.' A month later, on July 4, Thomas Jefferson stood before the Assembly and fearlessly read the momentous decision ever placed on paper. When he finished, the document was voted upon, accepted and signed by the fifty-six men, every one staking his own life upon his decision to write his name. Their decision insured the success of Washington's armies, because the spirit of that decision was in the heart of every soldier who fought with him and served as a spiritual power which recognizes no such thing as failure."

After the court hearing, it took another year before all the creditors were paid in full, with 8% interest, leaving a decent surplus for the shareholders. All that was left to be done was for the administrator to proceed to dissolve the company and bring this matter to an end. The matter had taken four years to reach this point. It was still far from over.

PERSISTENCE

> *"Persistence is to the character of man*
> *what carbon is to steel."*
>
> Napoleon Hill

Surrender Is Not an Option.

By mid-2011, almost a year after the court case, the administrator had paid off all the creditors, remitted the surplus monies to the shareholders, and settled his accounts. Before writing to the court to seek closure of the administration, the administrator had to proceed to dissolve the company with the Registrar of Companies House. Instead, at the last minute, the administrator's lawyer approached our lawyer stating that a party was interested to buy the shares of our company for £20,000.

I was stunned by this last minute offer. I knew in my gut that I had clearly missed a trick here. Over the past four years, I had learned a thing or two about my adversary. He was a cunning operator, who would never pay retail price for something he could get wholesale or even at cost. So, the fact that he was even offering this amount meant our shares had some serious value. I had to look into this matter.

After some research, I discovered that my adversary needed the shares of our company, because the import license in China for this one product was in the name of our company. If our company were to be dissolved, the Chinese import license, on which his entire business rested, would also expire, and as a result, his lucrative business would evaporate.

My decision was to commission a consulting firm to provide a valuation of the entire China business with respect to this product, whose import license was in the name of our company. The result was a significant valuation range. I resisted the urge to be greedy and chose to be reasonable so as to bring this matter swiftly to a close. I proposed to sell the shares for 10% of the lower amount of the valuation. The Chinese distributor rejected it without a counteroffer and threatened to sue the administrator if he proceeded to dissolve the company.

The administrator indicated to all sides that his decision was to seek a ruling from the court as to what he should do and submitted his paperwork to us. The hearing was scheduled in late 2012, but for technical reasons, it was moved to the spring of 2013.

In the fall of 2012, I was battle-weary, and my soul was parched. Like a deer looking for running streams, I needed spiritual refreshment, and so when the opportunity arose, I went on a pilgrimage to the Holy Land, with a group of friends, seeking enlightenment. I returned home, refreshed and revived, with an understanding that my problems were related to "control issues." My message was that I had to cede control of this matter to the Source. In retrospect, I had understood this message intellectually but had not grasped it emotionally. My spiritual journey had only started to gather speed.

There is no chivalry in war. The courts of law are in essence battlefields, where instead of weapons, words are used to win the battle of arguments. In fact, only a very small percentage of lawsuits end up in court, because of rising legal costs, wasted man-hours, and increased stress levels. Ours was one of these. We went to court in 2013, 2014, and 2015. I spent a great deal of money ramping up to each hearing, endless consultations with my solicitor and barrister, preparing documents, witnesses statements, and other submissions, and more money at the hearing itself, where I had a hard time stopping myself from biting my nails. My adversary used every conceivable excuse and reason to delay, divert, and distract the court so that these proceedings would exhaust us financially, mentally, and emotionally.

In my early years, I was never persistent. In fact, I was the opposite. I always preferred a swift solution to any problem, because I believed that time was more important than money. My mind was in the future: I lived for the future, and in a sense, I frittered away the present. Back in the mid-1990s, when I was a life insurance salesman, I read Napoleon Hill's *Think and Grow Rich* twice; one of the chapters that had a profound effect on me was "Persistence," and I have never forgotten his quote that "Persistence is to the character of man as carbon is to steel." I am certain that the reason I was able to withstand this ten-year litigation is down to this one chapter, and without it, I would not have had the awareness or the mind to persist for so long.

Yet, by December 2015, this case had drained me emotionally. In the afternoons, I found myself so exhausted that I was regularly taking naps. Talyn found this disturbing and insisted that I see the doctor, which I did. After looking at my blood test results, the doctor revealed that my testosterone and thyroid levels were on the lowest level possible. He asked what was going on in my life, and I told him the circumstances. He informed me that my body was telling me "enough is enough." So, despite the fact that my mind and spirit were willing to continue, my body could not. My doctor could prescribe medication to bring the testosterone and thyroid levels up, but if my stress levels continued, even these would prove futile. I could not force a settlement. Neither could I win, nor could I surrender. I had to exist in this trapped condition and not allow it to affect me, but I was at the end of my tether. Having fought this battle for almost a decade, surrender was not an option. I had to find another way.

Persistence is to the character of man as carbon is to steel. Success cannot be achieved unless a person is tested and overcomes the challenges as though by a baptism of fire. The basis of persistence is the power of the will.

There is no substitute for persistence. It cannot be replaced by any other quality. Those who have cultivated the habit of persistence seem to enjoy insurance against failure. No matter how many times they are defeated, they finally arrive at the top. Sometimes it appears that they have a hidden Guide whose job is to test men through all forms of discouraging experiences. Those who pick themselves up after a defeat and keep going on finally arrive at their destination, and the world applauds them. The hidden Guide lets no one enjoy great achievement without passing the persistence test. Those who can't "take it" simply do not make the grade. Those who can "take it" are bountifully rewarded for their persistence. Let's look at a few individuals who persisted and overcame overwhelming obstacles to achieve their dream.

Oprah Winfrey dealt with a lot throughout her public life – criticism about her weight, racism, intrusive questions about her sexuality, just to name a few – but she never let it get in the way of her ambition and drive. When you look at her childhood, her personal triumphs are even more remarkable.

Growing up, Oprah was a victim of sexual abuse and was repeatedly molested by her cousin, an uncle, and a family friend. Later, at age fourteen, she became pregnant and gave birth to a child, who passed away just two weeks later. But Oprah persevered, going on to finish high school as an Honors student, earning a full scholarship to college, and working her way up through the ranks of television, from a local network anchor in Nashville to an international superstar and creator of her own network.

J.K. Rowling had just gotten a divorce, was on government aid, and could barely afford to feed her baby in 1994, just three years before the first Harry Potter book, *Harry Potter and the Philosopher's Stone*, was published. When she was shopping it out, she was so poor she couldn't afford a computer or even the cost of photocopying the 76,944-word novel, so she persisted and manually typed out each version to send to publishers. It was rejected dozens of times until finally Bloomsbury, a small London publisher, gave it a second chance after the CEO's eight year-old daughter fell in love with it.

Steve Jobs was an American entrepreneur, business magnate, inventor, and industrial designer. He was the chairman, chief executive officer (CEO), and a co-founder of Apple Inc., and CEO of NeXt. Jobs is widely recognized as the leading pioneer of the micro-computer revolution of the 1970s and 1980s. He was fired from the company he founded – Apple. He also failed with NeXt Computer Company and the Lisa computer. When Jobs returned to Apple, he led the business to become the most profitable company in the US with the introduction of the ubiquitous iPhones and the unique Apple iMac computers.

What are the symptoms of lack of persistence?

The symptoms are self-evident, such as failing to clearly define what one wants, procrastination, lack of interest in specialized knowledge, indecision, self-satisfaction, indifference, blaming others, lack of desire, quitting at the first sign of difficulty, lack of planning, searching for shortcuts, and fear of criticism.

How does one develop persistence?

Hill suggests these four simple steps, which lead to the habit of persistence:

1. The definite purpose backed by a burning desire for its fulfillment.

2. The definite plan, expressed in continuous action.

3. The mind closed tightly against all negative and discouraging influences, including negative suggestions by relatives, friends, and acquaintances.

4. An alliance with one or more persons who will encourage one to follow through with both plan and purpose.

These four steps are essential for success in all walks of life, so make them a habit.

Finally, Hill shares with us a compelling point.

"I had the happy privilege of analyzing both Mr. Edison and Mr. Ford, year by year over a long period of years, and therefore the opportunity to study them at close range, so I speak from actual knowledge when I say that I found no quality save persistence, in either of them, that even remotely suggested the major source of their stupendous achievements."

The major source of their stupendous achievement is "persistence."

Surrender was not an option, so I sought and found another way from an unlikely source. For five years, I was a governor on the board of a leading Catholic girls' school in England, and I had the good fortune of knowing a nun, who had recently joined as a governor. The year before, she had retired after fifty years of service as a teacher in the school, and she was fearful about her future away from the place and people she loved. She had gone on a thirty-day silent retreat to rediscover herself and to discern what the Lord had in store for the next chapter in her life. Today, she runs the retirement home for her religious congregation with energy and enthusiasm and joined as a governor of the school she loved. Her story inspired me to rediscover myself and to discern what the Lord had in store for the next chapter in my life.

Following negotiations with my wife, I applied to join the thirty-day silent retreat in North Wales in the spring of 2016 and was delighted when they accepted my application.

9
SELF-IMAGE

*"The 'self-image' is the key to
human personality and human behavior."*

Dr. Maxwell Maltz

Meeting My Vulnerable Self

I arrived at the door of St Beuno's Jesuit Spirituality Centre near Rhyll, in North Wales, in the early evening of the 10th of January 2016. It was dark, cold, and raining, but nothing could get me down, as I felt energized at the prospect of getting to know who I truly was. A petite and elegant-looking nun, dressed in a green tartan skirt and a white blouse, opened the door for me and introduced herself as Sister Anne. In a few days, I would discover that she would be my spiritual director as I submerged myself in the silence of the rigorous thirty-day spiritual exercises or "examen," established by St. Ignatius, the founder of the Jesuit religious order.

During the first week, as I went slowly and deeper into the silence, I struggled not being able to speak with any of the other twenty-five persons on this retreat. There were several young Jesuit novices and mostly older men and women from all Christian denominations. I was fully aware that if this process was to work for me, I had to surrender to the process, which I did willingly. We had no access to mobile phones, computers, emails, televisions, radios, newspapers, magazines, or books, except for the Bible. The only time during the day in which I was able to speak was for thirty minutes, when I had my daily one-to-one with my spiritual director, Sr. Anne. That first week was the hardest.

During the second week, I chose to reflect on the houses that I had lived in throughout my life so as to elicit, from my deep memory, difficult events in my life as well as happy times. After drawing a mind map of these events, I wrote a journal of these incidents so that I could make some sense of them. What I discovered is that most of us accumulate as many as thirty personalities over time, from childhood. We then choose, fashion, and sculpt the strongest one as the personality to face the harsh world that we inhabit. Our hidden self, which is invariably the vulnerable one, is banished to a secret place, treated like a damaged relative – out of sight, out of mind. It is this vulnerable personality, my hidden self, I was seeking in the silent retreat, and I have now brought him out into the open and made friends with him. My self-image is changed and, as a result, so is my personality and behavior.

On the third week, to my surprise, I started to well up, and weep, in sadness over the harm and hurt I had caused others in my life. In the deep silence, all excuses and rationale for my actions abandoned me; it was as though it was futile to even try. In my mind's eye, I sat at the bottom of the deep end of a swimming pool, ostensibly able to breathe, and watch as all my excuses floated up toward the surface of the water. I was left exposed to the image of God within me, and it was as though I saw my sins as clear as daylight.

On the last week, I was still raw from the previous week's emotional and spiritual catharsis. I was still welling up often and at the slightest prompting; however, this week the emotion was not from sadness but from joy – an inexplicable joy. It was a joy of gladness, happiness, and lightness of being, as though all negativity in my life had been expunged. Now that I had felt, sensed, and touched the divine within me, I made a commitment that I would not return to my old way of life.

At first, I realized that I had never fully appreciated the beauty and joy of speaking in the moment, but by the last week of the retreat, I also realized that I had never really appreciated silence.

Many of these stories I am sharing were elicited during the silent retreat, and I am certain that without them, I could not have written this book.

My previous personality rears its head from time to time, but its days of supremacy are long gone. I had grown a beard in the silent retreat, and as a testament to my changed personality, I continue to wear a short beard as a daily reminder of my changed life. Thankfully, my wife and daughters prefer me this way.

"He will have difficulty in coping with university level exams."

In my early years, I slowly developed several different personalities at home in Khartoum. I behaved differently with my parents, my brothers, my cousins, my old school friends that still remained, the new friends I made at the American Club, my father's office employees, our Sudanese cook, servant, and maid, and so on.

At Douai School, my personality took on a new veneer, as I adapted to my new environment. My academic record was mediocre, at best. I worked sufficiently hard to pass exams and move on up to the next class. Working hard was unnatural for me, in my youth. My careers master, the late Fr. Terence, whose coffin I helped to carry at his funeral in November 2015, wrote in one of my school reports, which I still have, "He will have difficulty in coping with university level exams…he could aim for a Higher National Diploma in Business Studies. Academically that may prove the limit of his capabilities."

In retrospect, I recall being disappointed by that remark, and I am certain it impacted on my examination results, because at that time, in my mind, I had decided to agree with him. In any event, I pushed myself and was accepted at Bradford University Management Center, where I majored in Economics and Marketing.

Some fifteen years later, I rose to the challenge and opportunity, studied hard, and was accepted by New York University to do a Master's degree in Journalism. I felt vindicated. Had Fr. Terence not said that, perhaps I would not have had the need to prove anything. Fr. Bernard, my housemaster, whom I see each time I visit Douai, had more faith in me: he called me "an amiable achiever." I am grateful to both of them.

"Don't mess with George"

In my later years at school, my self-image took a turn for the better on the back of one event, a misunderstood event.

It was a Monday in late winter; dark clouds oppressed the skies, and rain poured relentlessly. Everyone, including me, looked miserable. I had just finished lunch and went to my dormitory to look for my Marlboro cigarettes so that I could have a smoke in the tennis shed. I looked under my bed, found the pack, opened it, and it was empty. I cussed under my breath.

Just then, John Norman, the largest and strongest boy in our class, and possibly in the school, who was also a formidable rugby player, came to my cubicle, and said, "George, do you have a fag? (English slang for cigarette), and I responded, "Sorry, Norm, I've run out too."

"You're such a liar, George," he said, "I know you have some hidden away."

"I don't have any, so just please leave me alone," I said irritated.

Norman refused to back away. He kept pushing me, again, and again, and again. Mondays were never my favorite days, and I was also on edge. I don't know exactly what happened, but as memory serves, I turned my body to the right, and suddenly out of nowhere, I lunged at Norman and landed a right fist on his face. I saw Norman's body go flying backwards about twenty feet. I watched in horror at what I had done and the impending consequences. A number of other boys, who were hanging around, also watched in disbelief.

Norman recovered and came charging at me like a water buffalo. My instinct kicked in, which was to save my prescription glasses. I took them off immediately and threw them on my bed a few feet away. As Norman was almost upon me, I swiftly bent my torso, curled my head and covered it with my arms, and shut my eyes, expecting to feel a great deal of pain. I felt Norman's body flip over my body and land with an enormous thud on the floor. As I turned around, opened my eyes, I saw Norman on the floor, whimpering in pain and one hand holding his shoulder.

I went over to him and tried to pull him up, but he was in pain. With the help of a few boys, we managed to slowly get him up, and we took him to the infirmary.

At supper that evening, the rumor was that George had thrashed Norman, and the evidence was Norman's left arm was in a sling. The whisper from ear to ear was: "Don't mess with George." All eyes were on me, and the eyes betrayed respect and fear. Although I tried not to show it, my heart and mind were surging with pride and power.

What was strange for me about this event was that I now had an enviable reputation, which I must say I enjoyed and milked it for what I could.

Dr. Maxwell Maltz, a cosmetic surgeon in New York in the 1970s and author of international bestseller *Psycho-Cybernetics*, discovered that although all his operations were on the surface successful, some of his patients showed no change in personality after surgery. In most cases, a person who had a conspicuously ugly face corrected by surgery experienced an almost immediate rise in self-esteem and self-confidence. But in some cases, the patient continued to feel inadequate and experienced feelings of inferiority. This indicated to Dr. Maltz that the reconstruction of the physical image itself was not the real key to changes in personality. After some time, he discerned that it was as if the personality itself had a face and that led him to explore this area. He discovered that self-image, the individual's mental and spiritual concept or picture of himself, was the real key to personality and behavior.

Dr. Maltz found his answers in the new science of cybernetics, which grew out of the work of physicists and mathematicians rather than psychologists. Any breakthrough in science is likely to come from outside the system, not from the experts in the field. Pasteur was not a medical doctor; the Wright brothers were not aeronautical engineers but bicyclists, and Einstein was not a physicist but a mathematician.

"The self-image is the key to human personality and human behavior. Change the self-image and you change the personality and behavior." Equally important is that the self-image sets the boundaries of individual accomplishment.

"The development of an adequate, realistic self-image will seem to imbue the individual with new capabilities, new talents, and literally turn failure into success."

The self-image is changed not by intellect alone or by intellectual knowledge alone but by "experiencing." Our self-image was developed by our past experiences. We can change it by the same method. When you "experience," something happens inside your nervous system and your midbrain, with new engrams and neural patterns being recorded in the gray matter of your brain. According to Dr. Maltz, this usually requires about twenty-one days to effect any perceptible change in mental image.

Most crucially, he advises that the most realistic self-image is to conceive of ourselves as "made in the image of God," and if we believe this, with full conviction, we cannot fail to receive a new source of strength and power.

William James, the father of American psychology, said that the power to move the world is in your subconscious mind. Whatever you impress on your subconscious mind, the latter will move heaven and earth to bring it to pass. You must therefore impress it with right ideas and constructive thoughts.

Dr. Joseph Murphy, a student of Neville Goddard and Dr. Maltz's, and author of *The Power of Your Subconscious Mind*, writes:

"The easiest and most obvious way to formulate an idea is to visualize it in your mind's eye, as vividly as if it were alive. Any picture, which you have in your mind, is the substance of things hoped for and the evidence of things not seen. What you form in your imagination is as real as any part of your body. The idea and the thought are real and will one day appear in your objective world, if you are faithful to your mental image."

You see, thinking forms impressions in your mind, and these impressions manifest themselves in your life as facts and experiences. A homebuilder will visualize the type of building he wants, and he sees it in his mind's eye in the way that he desires it to be completed. His imagery and thought processes become a plastic mold from which his building will emerge. Act as though you are, and you will be. In other words, a mental picture held in the mind, backed by faith, will come to pass.

Lastly, all this material is not new. In the Bible, St Paul recommends that we "pray continually and give thanks in all circumstances." (1 Thess. 5:18) Extraordinary results follow this simple prayer. The thankful heart, the heart full of gratitude, is always close to the creative forces of the Universe, causing countless blessings to flow toward it by the law of reciprocal relationship, based on cosmic law of action and reaction.

My surprise victory over John Norman impacted my fellow classmates. They saw me differently after that incident, and that changed how I saw myself. Although I was an unconscious competent in the arena of reputation, I had read Machiavelli's *The Prince*, and I knew I now had an edge, and I confess I did use it to my best possible advantage. In hindsight, I recognize that this experience was a clear finger post for me to pursue a career in various fields of "communications," such as marketing, public relations, journalism, writing, and public speaking.

However, at that time, the image I had on the outside did not correspond to the image on the screen of my mind. I did not feel like a true victor. At that time, I knew that I defeated John Norman by pure chance, not by physical strength.

Therefore, my internal dialog did not reflect the image that others saw of me. As an adolescent, victory by luck or stealth did not feel like a genuine victory. Today, I know better.

10
ATTITUDES

"The greatest discovery of my generation is that a human being can alter his life by altering his attitudes."

William James

Forgiveness Liberated Me

There have been a number of occasions in my life when my good will gestures and efforts, to family members, close friends, and especially business associates, have not only fallen on deaf ears, but I have felt the cold slap of ingratitude. Sometimes, I have expressed my feelings. Often, I have withdrawn to lick my wounds in private. On a few occasions, at traumatic junctures in life, like a death in the family, I have responded with fire and fury, much to my own amazement.

When my brother Simon died, on December 14, 2003, it was a terrible shock to everyone in our family. He was only forty-seven and had died from a massive heart attack. Simon left a widow and two teenage boys. On my mother's request, my brother Chris and I went to Toronto, Canada, to help his widow sort out Simon's estate. My father died four days later, so when we buried Simon, we returned to London to bury my father, before the year was out.

Our relationship with Simon's widow was a difficult one, and old resentments festered on both sides. There is no doubt that I was partly responsible for the difficulty in this relationship. We did what we could to help her, despite the unspoken coldness in the reception. Naturally, we wanted to help our nephews, in any way we could, and to be there for them when they needed advice from us.

Soon enough, we realized that our desire was a pipe dream, when we became aware that the resentments held by our sister-in-law and her eldest son were so deep. When the estate matter was completed, Chris and I made the difficult decision to withdraw so as not to exacerbate the situation. The negative vibrations we received were simply too toxic. This was one of the hardest decisions I have had to make, because it created a conflict between my strong sense of family unity and what I believed was the right thing to do. As I am a fervent believer in the laws of cause and effect, I am certain that this internal conflict was the cause that brought on my bone tumor and not just a random occurrence as my doctors had me believe.

I have always been an adventurer, an explorer, and an investigator, not only in the world outside me but also in the world within me. Several years after Simon's death and after my bone tumor episode, I spent three years in therapy, exploring my past to learn more about why I am who I am, and it was a most interesting journey, helping me to advance in my spiritual journey.

In May 2012, just as Talyn and I were about to fly to Venice on a short break, my business associate discovered a loophole in our agreement and saw an opportunity to take advantage of me and pressed to renegotiate our agreement. With my mind on this matter, I was unable to enjoy our holiday. After a tense and stressful three weeks of negotiations, I was compelled to reluctantly concede to many of his demands. I could not believe that a person I had helped extricate out of financial difficulties, could betray me so cold-heartedly. I was so over-whelmed with anger at his treachery that I found myself consumed with rage against him and against myself for coming to his aid in the first place.

After about six months, when the opportunity arose, I turned the tables on him, and I had him sign a new agreement with our original terms. Despite this, I found this feeling of rage within me every time I heard his voice or received an email from him was making me physically ill. I desired to keep him locked in a web of blame and guilt. I did not want to let him off the hook. Yet, it was I who was the prisoner. I knew this needed to stop. So one Friday evening, I decided that the next day, I would drive to Douai Abbey to see Fr. Nicholas Broadbridge, a Benedictine monk, who I knew gave "healing" workshops, and ask for his help.

That Saturday, after an hour's drive, I arrived at the Abbey at 10:10 am. As I entered the lobby, there was a notice on the wall that read, "Healing Workshop III – from 10 am to 4 pm. I was taken back by the coincidence and serendipity. I ventured into the room, where the workshop was being held and sat down at the back. When asked why I was there, I stood up and explained why. I think that all were surprised, including Fr. Nicholas. I listened and participated in the workshop, which was about "The Gifts of the Spirit."

After the workshop ended, Fr. Nicholas gave me time to talk to him about my rage, Fr. Nicholas said that I had to forgive my business associate for his treachery, in order to release this anger. I said that would not be possible. He replied that if that was my decision, no healing could take place. I did not want to carry this burden any longer, so I reluctantly conceded. He asked me to pray a special prayer asking Jesus to take this away from me and to heal me. I returned home that evening, in much lighter spirits.

In the following months, on different Saturdays, I attended another two healing workshops and a few one-to-one meetings with him. In the private meetings, he explained that we are all "wounded" at an early age, and he helped me to trace back my early memories. One significant memory of me as a child came back. I remember feeling abandoned at the age of seven at a nursery in Fribourg, Switzerland, where my parents had left me to go on a tour of Europe by car. Fear and anger came to mind, not love. Fr. Nicholas explained that my anger with my business associate was the "presenting problem," but the "real problem" lay in this earlier part of my life. He showed me how to pray to forgive my parents for what they had done; clearly, they had not meant to hurt me. I prayed to forgive them and to love them. He placed his hands on my head and we prayed together a special prayer for my parents, for my business associate, for my sister-in-law, and for me. By the end of that prayer, I felt as if a heavy weight had been lifted from me.

What is attitude?

Attitude is the composite of our thoughts, feelings, and actions. If we don't have a good attitude, whatever skill and talent we have will not be sufficient to achieve our goals. If you are mentally and physically in a bad vibration, that is all you can attract to you. Vibration is the law of the Universe, and we all live in an ocean of motion. We have the ability to choose. Our thoughts control our feelings, and our feelings control our actions. If we choose positive thoughts, these will control our feelings, which will control our actions. Your attitude is going to determine where you go in life; it's the foundation of failure and success.

Thomas Jefferson summed it up in two sentences. "Nothing can stop the man with the right mental attitude from achieving his goal. Nothing can help the man with the wrong mental attitude."

In his book *The Power of Awareness*, Neville Goddard writes a specific chapter on attitude. In it he states, "Since what we believe to be the 'real' physical world is actually only an 'assumptive' world, it is not surprising that what appears to be solid reality is actually the result of 'expectations' or 'assumptions.' The assumption of the wish fulfilled is a high tide which lifts you easily off the bar of the senses where you have so long lain stranded."

He narrates the story of a costume designer who described to him her difficulties with a prominent theatrical producer. She was convinced that he unjustly criticized and rejected her best work and was often deliberately rude and unfair to her. When Goddard questioned her, she confessed that every morning on her way to the theatre, she told him just what she thought of the producer in a way she would never have dared address him in person. The intensity and force of her mental argument with him automatically established his behavior toward her. When she realized what she had been doing, she agreed to change her attitude and to live this law faithfully by assuming that her job was highly satisfactory, and her relationship with the producer was a very happy one. To her great delight, she soon discovered that her attitude was the cause of all that befell her. The behavior of her employer miraculously reversed itself. His attitude, echoing, as it had always done.

In his audio recording of *Lead the Field*, Earl Nightingale, the American radio coach, said that attitude is the magic word. He also said that the single most valuable concept that he had learned was "an image of the mind," as represented by the "stick person." Originated in 1934 by Dr. Thurman Fleet, this drawing of a "stick person" gives one a model of what the mind looks like. There is a big circle and a small circle. The big circle represents the mind, and the small one represents the body. The big circle is cut in two, with the top half representing the conscious mind, the thinking mind, and the bottom half represents the subconscious mind, or the emotional mind. Any thought that you continuously impress upon your subconscious mind, over and over, becomes fixed in this part of your personality. The body is merely the instrument of your mind, and the thoughts that are consciously chosen and impressed upon the subconscious must move your body into action. As Nightingale explains,

> "Attitude is the reflection of a person. What's happening on the inside shows up on the outside. Our environment, the world we've created around ourselves, is really a mirror of our attitudes. If we don't like our environment, we can change it, by changing our attitudes. The easiest and most effective means of forming a good attitude habit is to begin conducting yourself as though you have a good, positive, expectant attitude toward life. If you've never tried it, you will be amazed at what happens. Remember that actions trigger feelings, just as feelings trigger actions."

The German philosopher Goethe put it this way, "Before you can *do* something, you must first *be* something."

More than anything else in the world, men, women, and children want and need more self-esteem. We all want to feel important, needed, and respected, and to the person who fills this need, they will give their love, affection, and respect. So, be that something. You may have noticed that the people with the best attitude naturally rise to the top.

Nightingale offers a few points to keep in mind:

1. Our attitude to any task will bring about its successful outcome.
2. Our attitude toward others determines their attitude toward us.

3. Before you can achieve the kind of life you want, you must think, act, and talk as would the person you wish to become.

4. Attitudes are not the result of success; success is the result of attitudes.

5. The deepest craving of human beings is for self-esteem: to be needed, to feel important, and to be appreciated.

Lastly, treat everyone you deal with as the most important person on earth. Start with this habit, practice it consistently, and you'll do it for the rest of your life.

When we forgive, we are doing ourselves a favor; we are not doing the other party a favor. When we hold resentments, we are not punishing the other party; we are punishing ourselves. When we are in a rage about someone, there is a warm and seductive feeling, which is illusory, and it is a form of dis-ease. When we forgive, it puts us at-ease. When I forgave my business associate and sister-in-law, I felt that forgiveness extinguished my anger, allowing me to breathe and to love again. When I say love, it is not a feeling I speak of but an act of will. We are not called to like these people, but we are called to love them. We do this for our own benefit, not theirs. To be able to forgive all injuries is the greatest gift we can bestow on ourselves, and what's more, it's a wonderful attitude.

Forgiveness is the sister of gratitude, so to show my gratitude, I helped Fr. Nicholas write, edit, and publish his book, *Our God Heals*.

I am always inspired by the wise words on gratitude of Mother Teresa of Calcutta, whose advice remains so eternal, so true and so uplifting:

"Some people come into your life as blessings, some come into your life as lessons.

If you want to change the world, go home and love your family.

God doesn't require us to succeed; he only requires that you try.

If you judge people, you have no time to love them.

Do things for people not because of who they are or what they do in return, but because of who you are.

Yesterday is gone; Tomorrow is not yet come; we have only today. Let us begin.

Every time you smile at someone, it is an action of love, a gift to that person, a beautiful thing.

Spread love everywhere you go.

If you can't feed a hundred people; feed just one.

Peace begins with a smile."

11
FEELINGS

"Not to expose your true feelings to an adult seems to be instinctive from the age of seven or eight onwards."

George Orwell

Love in a Fribourg Nursery

I remember when I first heard that President Kennedy was assassinated in Dallas, Texas, on November 22, 1963. I was eight years old, and it was on the car radio as I was being driven to school. Our Sudanese driver broke down in tears, and when I asked him what had happened, he told me and I too cried. This cannot be explained by logic or reason, but, to me, the emotional vibration over the radio waves was so strong, it had to be expressed.

Earlier that summer, my parents, two brothers, Simon and Jack, and I had traveled to Köln (Cologne), Germany, where my father had business with Bayer AG, whose agent he was in the Sudan, and while there, he purchased an *Opel Kadett Estate*. From Köln, we drove down toward Fribourg, Switzerland, where my parents placed us in a nursery managed by Benedictine nuns in their black habits. I still retain some strong memories from those days. One memory was seeing my mother wave goodbye to me, and I recall feeling very sad about it. Although I have no recollection of any feelings of anger or resentment, I am told that I must have had them. How is that possible? It is well understood in psychotherapy that children, being so dependent emotionally on their parents, will cover up for them, even to their own detriment. In my mind, I believe this is very plausible.

I remember a few events from those days. In one event, when the nuns took us for a walk in the woods with other children, we were instructed to pick only certain types of mushrooms, because some were poisonous. I also remember on another of these walks, where we were caught unexpectedly in a heavy storm, and I witnessed lightning strike a tree and fry it. As a result, we braved the rainstorm and pressed on to return to the house.

However, the story I want to share with you is of a brother and sister, who had some contagious disease and were confined in a house about a hundred yards away. The nuns instructed us to stay away from that house. That instruction to me was like a red rag to a bull.

One afternoon, when all the children and the nuns were busy getting organized to go on a walk, I slipped away and crawled commando-style through the grass toward the house. When I reached the house, I peeked through the first window and saw a bed with a young girl, in a white night-dress, sitting and reading. Then I saw another bed that was empty. With hands cupped around my temples, I looked around the room and saw a young boy playing on the floor. I knocked on the window to attract their attention, but they looked at me startled. I knocked again, and the boy slowly got up and came to the window. He and I pulled the window up sufficiently to allow me to slip through. I don't remember many details other than the fact that I did this regularly, and I sat on the girl's bed holding her hand. I became very attached to this girl. Ultimately, when my parents came to pick us up, I was reluctant to leave this girl. Whether real or imagined, my memory of my abandonment by my parents was now replaced by my abandonment of this girl.

"Sons and mothers, I sometimes think, is the greatest love story never told" wrote British journalist and television presenter Mariella Frostrup, in a 2018 article in *The Guardian* newspaper. She explains,

"In childhood, they are the perfect man, unconditionally loving and open to guidance and influence – almost every facet the opposite of the adult version. What woman wouldn't dote on such a creature, entirely portable and built for devotion?"

She describes the conflict endured by most teenage boys, between wanting to protect their mother and maintain their "special relationship" and dumping her for a teenage siren, which makes for amusing viewing, despite the element of heartbreak. "As with the melancholic Prince of Denmark, mothers remain a centrifugal force for far longer than most men deserve."

Undoubtedly, Mariella Frostrup has hit on a subject that is emotionally uncomfortable for men and women alike. There is clearly a connection between "the mother and son love story never told" and why men find it very difficult to express their feelings, and feelings is the subject of this chapter.

Consciousness is the one and only reality, and it is divided into two parts, the conscious and the subconscious, and we must understand the relationship between the two. The conscious mind is the thinking mind, and it is personal and selective. The subconscious mind is the emotional mind, and it is impersonal and non-selective. The conscious mind generates ideas and impresses these ideas on the subconscious; the subconscious receives ideas and gives form and expression to them. The conscious mind impresses on the subconscious mind, which then expresses.

In his book *Feeling Is the Secret*, Neville Goddard writes,

"Ideas are impressed on the subconscious through the medium of feeling. No idea can be impressed on the subconscious until it is 'felt' – it must be expressed. Feeling is the one and only medium through which ideas are conveyed to the subconscious…by control of feeling is not meant restraint or suppression of your feelings, but rather the disciplining of self to imagine and entertain only such feeling as contributes to your happiness."

So, we need to be careful of our moods and feelings, because there is a seamless connection between our feelings and our visible world. Our body is an emotional filter and bears the clear marks of our current emotions. It's not an exaggeration to say that a change of feeling is a change of destiny. Fate is not the author of our condition, and luck or accidents are not responsible for what happens to us. Our subconscious impressions determine the conditions of our world. "Whatever the mind of man can conceive and 'feel' as true, the subconscious can, must, and will objectify."

We must be aware that although the subconscious serves us faithfully, the relationship between the conscious and the subconscious is not one of master and servant but more like a woman one loves or a wife. The subconscious "has a distinct distaste for compulsion and responds to persuasion than to command."

Goddard writes, "The subconscious accepts as true that which you feel as true, and because creation is the result of subconscious impressions, you, by your feeling, determine creation." We are already what we want to be and our refusal to believe it is the only reason we do not see it. "To seek on the outside for that which you do not feel you are is to seek in vain, for we never find that which we want; we find only that which we are." How true is that? We make life so difficult by trying to be what we are not. If we only surrendered ourselves to be who we are, life energy would flow through us effortlessly and joyfully.

"It is only in sleep and in prayer, a state similar to sleep, that a person enters the subconscious to make his impressions and receive his instructions. In this state the conscious and subconscious are creatively joined. The male and the female become one flesh." Whatever we hold in our conscious minds as we drop off to sleep is the expression we receive when we wake up. So, it is crucial that we should always feel the wish fulfilled before we drop off to sleep. Remember, we never draw out of our deep self that which we want; we always draw out that which we are, and we are that which we feel ourselves to be.

"The feeling, which comes in response to the question 'How would I feel were my wish fulfilled?', is the feeling which should monopolize and immobilize our attention as we relax into sleep." Once we are asleep, we no longer have freedom of choice. Our mood prior to sleep defines the state of our consciousness.

"The subconscious never sleeps; it works twenty-four hours, seven days a week, from our birth to our death. Sleep is the door through which the conscious mind passes to be creatively joined to the subconscious. So, night after night, we should assume the feeling of being, having, and witnessing that which we seek to be or have. Our dreams take form as we assume the feeling of the reality. As soon as you succeed in convincing yourself of the reality of the state you are seeking, results follow to confirm your fixed belief. You cannot fail unless you fail to convince yourself of the reality of your wish.

"While you are awake, you are the gardener selecting the seeds for your garden. Your conception of yourself as you fall asleep is the seed you drop in the ground of the subconscious. What you take in as a feeling, you bring out as a condition or action. So sleep in the feeling of the wish fulfilled."

Now let's look at prayer. Earlier, we had mentioned that prayer is a state much like sleep. When we pray, we remove ourselves from the noise of the outside world, and we slowly drop into a state where we are more receptive to promptings from within. "Prayer is not so much what you ask for, as how you prepare for its reception."

In the Bible, there is a verse in Mark 11:24 which reads, "So I tell you, whatever you ask for in prayer, believe that you have received it, and it will be yours." Clearly, even Jesus taught, in no uncertain terms, that the only condition required is that you believe that your prayers are already answered. There is another unfashionable word for this state of mind and it is called "faith." Faith is feeling. You never attract that which you *want* but always that which you *are*.

"Prayer is the art of yielding to the wish and not forcing of the wish. All you can possibly need or desire is already yours. You need no helper to give it to you; it is yours now. Get into the spirit of the state desired, and call your desires into being by imagining and *feeling* your wish fulfilled."

My last memory of Fribourg was being in the back of the *Opel Kadett Estate*, and from the back window, waving good-bye to this girl in the white nightdress. Although, it may have been obvious to my mother what I was feeling, I did not share my feelings with her. Orwell was not exaggerating when he wrote, "Not to expose your true feelings to an adult seems to be instinctive from the age of seven or eight onwards." After Fribourg, I spent the next fifty years and more hiding my true feelings as best as I could. Now, like Paolo Coelho's hero in *The Alchemist*, "I see the world in terms of what I would like to see happen, not what actually does."

Some of the greatest inventions would not have happened if people chose to accept the world as it is. Great achievements and innovations begin with a mind-set that ignores the impossible. This is my true feeling now.

12
SUCCESS

*"Failures, repeated failures,
are finger posts on the road to achievement.
One fails forward toward success."*

C. S. Lewis

Crises are Opportunities

We generally recoil from the word failure and will do anything to avoid it. That is because most of us are so fearful of failure that we refuse to even try to succeed. We do not realize that we cannot reach success unless we are prepared to face repeated failures. It's such a pity, because in avoiding failure, we not only cheat ourselves, but also we miss out so much in life. I too was afraid of failure once but no more.

When I look back over the past sixty years of my life, I can now see the repeated failures that C S Lewis speaks of, and he was correct in saying that these repeated failures were finger posts on the road to achievement. Failures, for me, were events in my life that were emotional disappointments, disasters, and despairs, which in retrospect proved to be blessings in disguise. Yet, they were also the launch pads of my successes. The great Spanish mystic St. John of the Cross, author of the spiritual masterpiece and classic Christian masterpiece *Dark Night of the Soul*, called these turning points, "dark nights." He addressed the pain suffered in this world as slow openings to the things of God or, in today's language, painful experiences are the path to our growth.

My first disappointment was an emotional wrench – being sent away from the comfort of my home and family in the Sudan to boarding school in England. Yet this painful desolation bore fruit in that it provided me with an excellent English education, which formed a foundation for the rest of my life. Had I remained in the Sudan, I am certain that not only would I have had a poor education and been unprepared for the world I now inhabit, but I would also have developed into an entitled individual.

The next despair was what I have called my twilight trauma, when at the age of thirteen I was beaten up in my bed in the middle of the night in an open dormitory. I could have withdrawn and shriveled, but I did not. This experience also had two silver linings. First, it compelled me to face my fears head on, challenge them, and overcome them with my determination not to allow them to sink me and by my will to respond in action. The boys who beat me up were no more than a catalyst in my transformation. The result of this event was that it made me become a positive individual and a mental gymnast with words, learning new words each day, because I understood the power of words, and I could use them to respond to thwart my opponents.

At the age of twenty-one, instead of finding a world of excitement, joy, and possibilities, I discovered a world of scarcity, limitation, and fear. On returning home to the Sudan, I recognized that the life that I had envisaged living there was a mirage. My friends from the holidays were no longer there. Working in my father's business in the Sudan, while comfortable and on the face of it potentially lucrative, held no excitement for me, and I could not see a future there. Going to the US was a faraway dream and not even open for discussion.

After two years in the Sudan, I returned to London, and the job prospects were not alluring, so I took what I was offered and worked in drawing up export contracts at Tennant Guaranty in the City of London. My relationship with Jane took a turn for the worse, when Alex, my friend and her brother, was killed in a car accident in Somalia. I found my world spiraling downwards, oppressed by dark clouds, mirroring my emotional state. I was forlorn, and my mood was dark.

Yet, paradoxically, these dark and difficult days were essential passages for me. In the process, I also learned that one cannot trifle with relationships; they are sacred. What you put in is what you get out. Once you make a commitment, you must stick with it, because if you don't, you will pay the price, and believe me, the price is very steep.

In retrospect, I realized that this difficult stage in my early life was the prelude to my new life, a life I thought could no longer be mine: a life I did not think I deserved. My life took a new turn, after my eight-mile run to Wimbledon, when I began to get to know Talyn, and not long afterwards, we married. I call her "the woman of my dreams," because she supported my dream of living and working in the US, and quite auspiciously, she was born on the 4th of July – serendipity or what? All things are one way or another working for our good, by helping us to find God.

The next challenge was the closure of our furniture business in New Jersey, which was also a blessing in disguise, because it released us from the tedium of running a business, which we no longer believed was part of our future. We sold our offices in the summer of 1987, a few months before the October market crash, at a substantial profit, because we had converted it from a residential home. The sale price of the office recouped most of our investment in the furniture business. We now had the time we needed to save and secure the commercial property of my parents, who were struggling under the financial pressure exerted by their managing agent. This event gave me – and my brother Chris – the confidence we needed. It also gave me the opportunity to show how I could execute a plan from start to finish and secure victory. It was a wonderful and exhilarating moment but far too short-lived.

After this matter was resolved, I slowly lost interest in property management, but the money was good, so I was reluctant to let it go. Ultimately, I did, and went on to study journalism at New York University, which was hard, but I am grateful for the opportunity it gave me.

Going down the narrow path, even when you know it is the right thing to do, is difficult, especially when you know that you have left behind the easy road. It gave me a fresh perspective as to why the Hebrews were complaining about how they missed the good times in Egypt, after Moses had led them into the Sinai desert, where water and food were scarce. Yet, if I had not taken this difficult road, I would not have produced the ten books that I have written over the past two decades. The obstacles are not barriers; the obstacles are the way. They are actually our life-path.

When I think of the perfect storm that hit my life in 2007 – the house move, the death of Talyn's father, and my bone tumor – this was truly a time of despair, but somehow, someway, we managed to meander through it and survived. Yes, it did take six months to recuperate, but given that I was facing death, that seemed a very small price to pay. I have no regrets and recriminations about this event. In fact, I am so grateful that it happened, because it was my wakeup call. I do not take life for granted anymore. Every day is a gift, a bonus.

Having cheated death, I faced another difficult decision that would change the course of my life and test me as never before. I have always been a dealmaker, a strong believer in win-win scenarios, because I believed that I am a fair and reasonable person, and because I believe that time is money. Yet, Providence had different plans for me. He gave me this experience to compel me to endure, resist, and persist. If you cannot have a win-win scenario, and surrender is not an option, because it means you will lose it all, you are compelled to fight on, and on, and on, until you secure victory, but I had no control over the timetable.

I did not have control over the timetable on negotiations, which are still ongoing as I write, but I did have control over what I wanted to do with my life. After attending Bob Proctor's weeklong seminar and completing his "Thinking Into Results" program over six months, my life has been transformed, and I am growing on so many levels. I am now so happy and grateful to be a writer and speaker on the topic of gratitude, the single most important practice in life.

One of the most difficult things to change is one's self-image. At school, my careers master wrote in a report that I "will have difficulty in coping with University level exams." Instead of crushing me, it pushed me to prove him wrong. My Myers-Briggs Type indicator showed my personality as borderline between leader and teacher. For much of my life, I have been a leader, a fighter, if you will, but now after this decade of litigation, I have matured and ripened, and my personality has moved more toward the teacher mode. As one feels on the inside, so it is reflected on the outside.

Along with my change of self-image, a change also occurred in my emotions. With leadership, one experiences treachery, which is difficult to forgive, and over time, it can drive one toward anger and resentment, which only punishes one's self, not the betrayer. Therefore, reluctantly, I have had to forgive those who have betrayed me, so as to let go of the anger that was punishing me.

Next, the most important and most misunderstood feeling is "love." Our inability to love is rooted in our childhood, and we are all wounded, in one way or another in childhood. For many, but not all, it takes the rest of our lives to recalibrate it. It is the human experience. After several years of therapy, several healing workshops, thirty-day silent retreats, and so on, I can, with some certainty, state that my wound is abandonment, and as a result, when I am let down, I react with anger. Now, I know and understand that my wound, my vulnerability, is also the seat of my power, and with this knowledge that I share with you, I am able to shed light on my dark side and yours. Carl Jung said, "We have two destinies, one spiritual, and pre-scripted and one karmic, and self-scripted. And not until we align our two destinies will we find the pearl of great price. This is the mystery of our becoming."

Lastly, as C S Lewis put it so eloquently, "Our failures, repeated failures, are the finger posts on the road to achievement. One fails forward to success." From my perspective and experience, I can vouch that success is the offspring of our failures. I would have it no other way, and I am so happy and grateful for all the rich blessings – positive and negative – that life has thrown at me.

When life throws us difficult times, we do not always have to resist and fight at all costs. We need to discern the situation, assess the pros and cons, and make a decision. We might choose to fight or to let go, and whatever we decide is the right decision for us.

We need to be able to recognize failure symptoms in ourselves so that we can do something about them. We need to become "aware" of them and recognize them as things that we do not want. Above all, we must convince ourselves deeply and sincerely that these things do not bring us happiness. No one is immune to negative feelings and attitudes. Even the most successful personalities experience them at times. The important thing is to recognize them for what they are, and take positive action to correct course.

We must differentiate our "self" from our "behavior." We are neither ruined nor worthless because we made a mistake. We must not hate ourselves because we are not perfect. No one else is either, and those who try to pretend are fooling themselves.

This urge to be important is universal, and we must be so, but we make a mistake when we seek it in conformity, in the approval of other people, or in material things. We are a gift of God, and we must give ourselves permission to be who we are meant to be. What you seek is seeking you, so have faith and follow your dream.

It is not events that age us but our emotional reactions to them. Many men sleepwalk into retirement, and then they go downhill rapidly. They feel that their active, productive life is completed, and their job is done. They have nothing to look forward to, so they become bored, inactive, and often suffer a loss of self-esteem, because they are no longer needed. A great many of them die within a year or so of retirement. Those who recognize that retirement is an industrial age word, which does not apply to our era, can carve themselves a new life. By being emotionally prepared, they can create a new, fulfilling, and rewarding life, which will give them purpose, self-esteem, and a longer and healthier life.

Science and faith have a challenging relationship, but they are opposite sides of the same coin. If we are to get more out of life, we should not limit ourselves to one or the other, because we need them both. The most realistic self-image is to conceive yourself as "made in the image of God." If you deeply and sincerely believe that you are made in the image of God, it is impossible not to receive a new source of strength and power.

In his book *The Power of Awareness*, Goddard, writes a chapter on "Failure," and I have extracted one crucial point about the importance of being "natural," if one is looking for success.

"The fact that it does not feel natural to you to be what you imagine yourself to be is *the secret of your failure*. If you do not feel *natural* about what you want to be *you will not be it*."

How can this secret of naturalness be achieved?

"The secret lies in one word – *imagination*. The essential feeling of naturalness can be achieved by persistently *filling your consciousness with imagination* – imagining yourself being what you want to be or having what you desire. What you truly and literally must feel is that with your *imagination, all things are possible*. You must realize that changes are not caused by caprice, but by a change of consciousness. If your assumptions are not fulfilled it is because of some error or weakness in your consciousness. However, these errors and weaknesses can be overcome. And remember that the time it takes your assumption to become reality is proportionate to the naturalness of being it."

So, let us imagine and truly feel that what we seek is not only possible but also believe that we have already received it.

CONCLUSION

When you visit the Grand Canyon in Arizona, you cannot but marvel at the enormity of its size and its breathtaking magnificence. Elizabeth Kubler-Ross once said, "Should you shield the canyons from the windstorms, you would never see the beauty of their carvings." Much like the carvings on the canyons, the challenges and difficulties that have been carved in our lives are blessings, because they have defined and shaped us and make us who we are today. Therefore, we must be grateful for them and count our blessings.

I share with you a few ideas that will change how you look at things. Wayne Dyer once said, "If you change the way you look at things, the things you look at change." It's another way of saying that if you rewire your brain, what you see will be different.

In *Insight* magazine of Smith College, a leading liberal arts college in Massachusetts, Carol Zaleski, professor of world religions there, writes, "Gratitude, it seems, is a universal phenomenon, an impulse hardwired in human nature... For Christians, the Eucharist (from the Greek word for thanksgiving) is the central liturgical act... for Muslims, the Quran is an ever-present reminder that our existence is a sheer gift, and Ramadan is a full month of gratitude... for Buddhists, gratitude is the main currency of the "economy of gift" that binds monastics to householders... for Hindus, gratitude finds expression in countless small acts of hospitality and service toward the divine presence in the household or temple shrine."

There is a saying that "Time is money." For many years, I believed this to be true, and I applied it to my working life. Now, I know that saying was wrong, because "Time is *not* money: Time is everything." So, don't waste your time on anger and resentment, spite, or envy. Think of how precious and irreplaceable your time is today. Always move positively forward, no matter how you feel. You may be exhausted, discouraged, and uncomfortable, but stay the course.

Investing in myself was not always a priority in my life, but in January 2016, I was at the end of my tether, when I was compelled to go and seek direction for my life. As I recounted earlier, I went to a silent retreat in North Wales to spend thirty days in silence and solitude to reflect: to audit the blessings and challenges in my life that have shaped me. The silence and the solitude were especially effective and productive for me. The time I invested in reflection, prayer, and study reaped a rich harvest, a harvest of stories, which you have read in this book. This harvest also showed me that all the challenges and difficulties in my life have also been the springboards for all the blessings that I have received. Without the challenges and difficulties, no blessings would or could have materialized for me.

I have often discovered that when I fail to get what I want, it may just be a blessing in disguise because something better is around the corner. Two years ago, I wrote a book on my spiritual journey, which featured many of these stories in this book, but it was rejected and never published. Naturally, I was disappointed and dejected. Now, I am so grateful that book was never published, because these stories are featured in this book. In the end, everything works for the best.

When we find it impossible to accept life as it presents itself at the moment, we make ourselves unhappy. We cannot calm the storm, so we must stop trying. What we can do is to calm ourselves until the storm passes, and it will, because nothing is permanent. When we understand this, we can do almost anything we want, because we have let go. The most powerful changes happen when we take control over what we can do, instead of craving control of what we cannot do.

There are no permanent jobs on this earth; we are all interns here. Learn from everyone, remain humble, and enjoy yourself. You cannot change others; you can only change yourself. If you don't like the results you are getting, change your habits and behavior, and your results will change. Remember each and every day is a new beginning, and the possibilities are endless. Be strong enough to let go, wise enough to move forward, and patient enough to wait for the results you deserve.

Gratefulness is a paradox. The cup of gratitude is always full, so you need add nothing. "The very shape of zero, written as 0, expresses emptiness. But the full circle also signifies fullness," writes Brother David Steindl-Rast. "Zero stands for nothing, but by adding zero to a number we can multiply it tenfold, a hundredfold, a thousandfold. Gratefulness gives fullness to life by adding nothing. Understanding 0 by becoming 0 – that's what gratefulness is all about." It is almost like seeing a Universe in an atom. The concept of gratefulness is a paradox, because by adding nothing, we become so rich. Why would we not want to live in this true paradox?

I hope that in these pages, you will have seen that some of the challenges I faced in my life were actually blessings in disguise and launch pads to my joys, happiness, and successes. Crises are opportunities. And I pray that you will give yourself the time to audit your life, to discover your challenges and your joys and successes so that you recognize that "gratitude is heaven itself."

ACKNOWLEDGEMENTS

My first debt of gratitude is to Sandy Gallagher, whose gratitude session at the Matrixx event in August 2017 opened my eyes to the power of gratitude and how practicing gratitude uplifts our vibrations and opens us up to accept our difficulties, to harness the good from it, and to forgive the rest.

I thank Bob Proctor, my mentor, and all who work with the Proctor Gallagher Institute, for their friendship and support.

Enormous thanks go to my Matrixx Mastermind Team – MaryAnn Kerubo, Lynn Rossi, Joan Ryan, Peggy Hoover, Kim Sykes, and Matt Curfman – for their invaluable time, gentle encouragement, and thoughtful assistance, especially when things were not going well for me.

My sincere thanks go to Peggy McColl and her team at Best Seller Maker for enthusing me to write yet another book; to Judy O'Beirn and her team at Hasmark Publishing for their professionalism in putting this book together for me; and most especially to my editor, Sigrid Macdonald, for her scrupulous and outstanding editing; and to Anne Karklins for her impressive use of her imagination and intuition in designing an extraordinary book cover.

I would like to extend my special gratitude to the Abbot and monks at Douai Abbey, especially to Fr. Finbar for his hospitality as guest master, to Fr. Nicholas for his healing workshops that feature in this book, and to Fr. Bernard, my gentle old housemaster, who has also been a longtime mentor to me.

I am most grateful to all my mentors, dead or alive, who have guided and inspired me from my earliest years: Emma and Onnik Kaloustian of the Armenian School in Khartoum; Mr. Desmond Cullen, my English teacher at Assumption House in Ramsgate, Kent; Fr. Alphonsus Tierney OSB, the headmaster at Douai School, and my English teacher, along with Mr. William Bell; Fr. Bernard Swinhoe OSB, my gentle housemaster, who showed me the power of servant leadership; Mr. Pearson, my History teacher; Mr. Peter Moore, my French teacher; Dr. Sparkes, my Economics professor at Bradford University Management Centre; Prof. Richard Cunningham, Prof. Stephen Solomon, Prof. Marcia Rock, Prof. David Dent, and Prof. Michael Norman at the Graduate School of Journalism, New York University; Bill Russell, Adrian Barrett, Gill Cons, Mike Silverman, and Kate McNeilly from various Toastmasters clubs in London; my spiritual directors, Canon Stuart Wilson, Fr. Dermot Power, Fr. Michael Mullan, and Sr. Anne Morris; Victor Abagi, who taught me for two years how business was conducted in the Sudan; George Kassabian, my maternal uncle and business mentor for five years in London; and John W. Rick III, fundraising consultant and friend, who, over the past decade, taught me everything I know about fundraising and alumnae development.

Finally, I am thankful to my late father-in-law, Avo, for his wisdom; to my late mother-in-law, Seta, for her warm hospitality over the years at her home; to my late father, Edward, whose warmth and generosity I miss dearly; to my mother, Molly, who is ninety-one this year, for her moral compass; and last but surely not least, to Talyn, for her love and unstinting support of me, through thick and thin, over the past thirty-five years.

ABOUT THE AUTHOR

George Jerjian graduated with a business degree from Bradford University in England (1973) and a master's degree in Journalism from New York University (1993). He has worked as a Chartered Marketer for the past 40 years, as partner in a US commercial real estate venture for the last 30 years, as a writer of 10 books over the last 20 years, and as a speaker for the last 15 years, earning the Distinguished Toastmaster award in 2013. He now devotes his time to consulting, coaching, speaking and writing.

OTHER BOOKS BY GEORGE JERJIAN

Seven Ages; Personal Financial Planning (1997)

The Battle of the Portals (1999)

Ecosystem: Living the 12 Principles of e-Business (2001)

Xerox Firestorm (2001)

The Truth Will Set Us Free: Armenians and Turks Reconciled (2003)

Sarkis Izmirlian: A Biography (2008)

Seeking God: A Pilgrimage in the Holy Land (2013)

Arabkir (2014)

Daylight After a Century (2015)

www.georgejerjian.com
www.spiritofgratitude.com

Hearts to be Heard
Giving a Voice to Creativity!

Wouldn't you love to help the physically, spiritually,
and mentally challenged?

Would you like to make a difference
in a child's life?

Imagine giving them:
confidence; self-esteem; pride; and self-respect.
Perhaps a legacy that lives on.

You see, that's what we do.
We give a voice to the creativity in their hearts,
for those who would otherwise not be heard.

Join us by going to
HeartstobeHeard.com
Help us, help others.

Printed in Poland
by Amazon Fulfillment
Poland Sp. z o.o., Wrocław